Naghmeh Varghaiyan & Karam Nayebpour

# Storytelling as an Act of Remembering
Episodic Memory in Post-Millennial Irish Narrative

Naghmeh Varghaiyan & Karam Nayebpour

# STORYTELLING AS AN ACT OF REMEMBERING
Episodic Memory in Post-Millennial Irish Narrative

**Bibliografische Information der Deutschen Nationalbibliothek**
Die Deutsche Nationalbibliothek verzeichnet diese Publikation in der Deutschen Nationalbibliografie; detaillierte bibliografische Daten sind im Internet über http://dnb.d-nb.de abrufbar.

Bibliographic information published by the Deutsche Nationalbibliothek
Die Deutsche Nationalbibliothek lists this publication in the Deutsche Nationalbibliografie; detailed bibliographic data are available in the Internet at http://dnb.d-nb.de.

Cover picture: Unsplash / Jeremy Bishop

ISBN-13: 978-3-8382-1856-4
© *ibidem*-Verlag, Stuttgart 2023
Alle Rechte vorbehalten

Das Werk einschließlich aller seiner Teile ist urheberrechtlich geschützt. Jede Verwertung außerhalb der engen Grenzen des Urheberrechtsgesetzes ist ohne Zustimmung des Verlages unzulässig und strafbar. Dies gilt insbesondere für Vervielfältigungen, Übersetzungen, Mikroverfilmungen und elektronische Speicherformen sowie die Einspeicherung und Verarbeitung in elektronischen Systemen.

All rights reserved. No part of this publication may be reproduced, stored in or introduced into a retrieval system, or transmitted, in any form, or by any means (electronic, mechanical, photocopying, recording or otherwise) without the prior written permission of the publisher. Any person who does any unauthorized act in relation to this publication may be liable to criminal prosecution and civil claims for damages.

Printed in the EU

In memory of Fati Sedighzadeh, an excellent mother

# Acknowledgements

The idea of this book came to us during our summer holiday in Europe in 2022. Based on a pre-established 'reading-while-travelling' list, we were reading some post millennial narratives from contemporary Irish literature. We read many works, but were thrilled by *The Sea* while in Viborg, Aarhus, Denmark. For this, we owe warm thanks to Nima, for his generous hospitality. We read *The Gathering* during our two-week stay in Zurich, at our uncle's in Rekingen. We owe our heartily thanks to Behrouz, Monica, and their lovely family for their companionship. We read *Milkman* in many places. For this, we owe thanks to many unnamed people. The main part of this book was written during our two-week winter stay at 17 Shahrivar Street in Tabriz, Iran. The tranquillity of the place encouraged us to think over what we had read many times. For this, we wish to thank to Aziz Maman, Day Day, Alireza, Zahra, Mesut, Akram, Azam, Buyuk Agha, Amir, Nasrin, Ali, Someyye, and Ilia. This book took its final form in our offices at Agri Ibrahim Cecen University, Türkiye. We are thankful to our students and colleagues. Above all, we owe thanks and gratitude to Father Farhad, for his lifelong curiosity and desire for reading and for Mother Fati, for her natural and eternal kindness. In all steps of this work, Nihal and Nilay were our lovely companions. We are happy to share our memories with them.

# Preface

Storytelling is as old as human beings. Our mind processes the world through stories; they make the world meaningful for us. As a natural innate skill and disposition, storytelling connects us to other times as well as to other people. We re-experience our past lives and experiences through recollecting and retelling them. The past is an ever-flowing and a never-dying river in human consciousness. Any single piece of our memories is a constituent part of this river. By our acts of remembering, we continuously and intermittently become connected to this river of consciousness. Therefore, remembering is an integrated part of our mind. Similarly, it is a salient property of fictional minds too. The past is a defining element for characters' sense of identity in narrative fiction.

The fact that our sense of identity is continuously formulated as stories ensure its continuity from the past to the future. Memory plays an important role in the construction, presentation, and processing of stories. If read from this perspective, more than anything else, (narrative) literature is about remembering, retrieving, recollecting, retelling, and re-experiencing. Fictional characters mostly share with their audience their memories themselves and about others too. Based on what they remember, they comment on themselves, on other people, and related events. Storytelling is, therefore, a dialogic activity since through it the characters enter a sincere dialogue with themselves and with others.

Storying the past based on experienced and invented memories lies at the heart of the narratives analysed in the present book. *The Sea* (2005) by John Banville, *The Gathering* (2007) by Anne Enright, and *Milkman* (2018) by Anna Burns are post-millennial Irish narratives in which remembrance of the things past is indexed to the first-person narrators' sense of identity. In its three parts, this book tries to show how the remembering of eventful episodes from the past has some emotional and cognitive advantages for the storytellers.

Naghmeh Varghaiyan & Karam Nayebpour<br>May 2023 / Agri-Türkiye

# Table of Contents

Acknowledgements .......................................................................... 7

Preface ............................................................................................. 9

Table of Contents ......................................................................... 11

**ONE**
**INTRODUCTION** ........................................................................ 13

**TWO**
Shadow of the Past: Narration and the Creation of Memory in John Banville's *The Sea* ............................................................ 27

    2.1   The Ontological Functions of Remembering ................... 31

    2.2   Max Morden's Struggle with his Fading Memory .......... 40

**THREE**
Fictions of the Past: Memory and Imagination in Anne Enright's *The Gathering* ........................................................ 49

    3.1   Remembering as an Act of Memory Formation .............. 58

    3.2   Veronica Hegarty's Forging of Identity through Memory Patches ............................................................... 67

**FOUR**
Mirror of the Past: Narrator as Rememberer in Anna Burns's *Milkman* ....................................................................................... 79

    4.1   Remembering as a Reliable Medium of Retelling (History) ............................................................................. 89

    4.2   The Unnamed Rememberer's Struggle against the Social Mind's Definition of Her Identity ................. 103

**FIVE**
**CONCLUSION** ........................................................................... 117

WORKS CITED ........................................................................... 123

About the Authors ...................................................................... 129

# ONE
# INTRODUCTION

> "[S]uppose I wholly lose the memory of some parts of my life, beyond a possibility of retrieving them, so that perhaps I shall never be conscious of them again; yet am I not the same person, that did those actions, had those thoughts, that I was once conscious of, though I have now forgot them?"
> (John Locke 342)

> "Memory is the most important epic faculty of all."
> (Walter Benjamin 62)

> "[M]aybe retellings have over-rounded it into a story."
> (Julian Barnes 62)

Irish voice is loud and sharp in English and world literature. The distinctive qualities of Irishness are best represented in Irish literature practiced by Irish writers within the borders of Ireland. The country, in Liam Harte's words, "has, since the late nineteenth century, produced a roll call of distinguished literary novelists and short story writers whose collective contribution to world literature has been far out of proportion to the country's size and population" ("Modern" 3). The inquiring, ironic and satiric nature of the Irish voice has been an integral part of English literature since Jonathan Swift's *A Modest Proposal* (1729).

In terms of the concerned narrative issues in Irish literature, a gradual change has occurred since the modernist era of literature. The formative influence of Samuel Beckett and James Joyce on Irish novelists' formal and thematic practices is a universally acknowledged fact (Harte, "Modern" 3)[1]. By widely using modernist narrative techniques, in a similar way to Joyce, contemporary Irish novelists mainly represent the problem of self/identity through the narration and/or remembrance of things past. In other words, the

---

[1] In his conversation with Mike Murphy, the contemporary Irish writer John Banville holds that "The 'two great novelists' of the century have been Joyce and Beckett. Joyce put everything in and Beckett threw everything out. [...] What novelists like myself try to do is put everything in, then throw it out, and deny it, and do both things at the same time" (qtd in Fibrate 60).

implementation of narrative techniques and strategies widely used by the modernist writers, such as internal focalization, allow contemporary Irish novelists to recount their memory-driven narratives by focusing on the long-term impact of some particular events in the past on the central characters' minds, and sense of subjectivities.

Post-millennial Irish fiction, according to Susan Cahill, brought a "new fictional renaissance" (603). This literary revival[2] was one aspect of the overall innovation in Irish society. "One of the key concepts of the millennium," as Cahill highlights, "was the idea of the new. The opening years of the century revealed an Ireland that, in many ways, was radically different to the country of just twenty years earlier. Here was a changed nation [...] that bore little similarity to the conservative, inward-looking society of previous decades" (604). Along with socio-cultural changes, "the opening two decades of the twenty-first century," argues Cahill, "have witnessed an extraordinary renaissance in Irish fiction, featuring novels that are stylistically experimental, ethically engaged, and pointed in their social, cultural, and political critiques" (618).

In *The Sea* (2005) by John Banville, *The Gathering* (2007) by Anne Enright, and *Milkman* (2018) by Anna Burns, the narrators, on the one hand, recount, retell, imagine, or re-experience some traumatic events in their past and, on the other hand, they present the long-term effects of the represented and/or reconstructed events on their sense of identity at the time of narration. In other words, the examined narratives are both about the objects of experience in the past as well as the identity of the experiencing subjects at the time of narration. The deeply traumatized narrators break their silences about some momentous events in their past after a long time. In this sense, they follow the Irish literary tradition since, as Anne

---

[2] Such a sociocultural change resonates with Ezra Pound's (1885–1972) slogan 'Make It New' which, according to Bledsoe "compels the writer to create out of the material of art work that is distinctively innovative. The artist must break with the formal and contextual standards of their contemporaries in making works fundamentally individual. These 'new' modern works cannot be wholly autonomous, however, as they must consider the aesthetics of the past in the context of the present moment."

Enright states, "Traditionally, Irish writing has been about breaking silences" (qtd. in Jordan). Besides that, what the contemporary Irish writer Colm Tóibín in his interview with Lisa Guidarinias argues is also true about the analysed narratives, "There is a lovely strangeness about Irish writing, an unpredictability, and a way of handling solitude and dark themes."

Recounting remembered acts through internal focalization provides the writers, in T. S. Eliot's terms, with an "objective correlative"[3] to represent the emotional aspect of their art. Similarly, the episodic recounting acts in the examined narratives provide the narrators with an effective tool to tell the story of what happened to them in the past, and also what they think and how they feel about it at the time of narration. Thus, in the three analysed narratives, the act of remembering, which in Astrid Erll's words is "always an 'anachronic process'" (214), has potential to evoke similar emotions in the reader. The goal of remembering in them is mostly therapeutic. As Kathleen Costello-Sullivan states, "many more recent contemporary Irish novels redirect their energies away from past trauma and toward a narrative recreation of the process of recovery, with a refocus on recuperative potentialities" ("Trauma" 408). The theme of recuperation also runs through the acts of memory in the examined narratives wherein the narrators' remembering and retelling acts are interwoven with their performance of them.

The three post-millennial Irish narratives in this study are prototype examples which represent the way literature has the potential to deal with personal wounds and transform traumatic experiences into memorable stories through retelling them. They are narratives of and about memory. The plotlines in these narratives turn around the positive effects of storying the traumatic episodes.

The traumatic past, damaged selves, dysfunctional families, lack of individual autonomy and the conflict between self and other

---

[3] According to Eliot, "The only way of expressing emotion in the form of art is by finding an 'objective correlative'"; in other words, a set of objects, a situation, a chain of events which shall be the formula of that particular emotion; such that when the external facts, which must terminate in sensory experience, are given, the emotion is immediately evoked" (145).

are among the shared themes in these narratives. Above all, their joint primary concern, which is also the main subject of the present book, is their focus on the central narrator-characters' acts of remembering and their sense of identity. The remembering narrators have retained some traces of their autobiographical memories. They reconstruct their sense of identity through the process of remembering some parts or episodes from their histories. The remembered acts of their past are framed by their more experienced selves at the time of narration.

Memory, in Endel Tulving's and Fergus Craik's definition, "is usually thought of as the ability to recollect past events and to bring learned facts and ideas back to mind" (v). Memory also plays a defining role in human identity. In other words, as Grmusa and Oklopcic emphasise, "our memories — our reinterpretations of past experiences, cultural contexts, and national his-stories — frame our identity and constitute our subjective selfhood" (1). In its sense of recollecting ability as well as formation or construction of identity, memory, in *The Sea*, *The Gathering*, and *Milkman*, is a personified basic narrative element. It is represented as an organic entity which is not lost through time. Rather, it changes into the central part of the characters' identity. The three narratives are thus the narrators' narratives of identity which mainly depends on the narration and remembrance of the past events as much as on the interpretation and evaluation of them.

The main reason behind the narrators' strong desire to tell their stories is to find a way to go beyond the restricting impact of the past. The unavoidable need for remembering is a significant shared quality in the analysed narratives where some episodes from the past are continuously in the process of recreation in the narrators' minds. The remembering first-person narrators try to vividly recollect and recount mostly the painful events in their past lives. A traumatic event lies at the centre of each of their personal (hi)stories. By focusing on their trauma-afflicted old selves, the narrators share with us their thoughts and feelings about what happened in their far past and how they interpret this after a long time. To do so, they necessarily tell us a story because "Remembering an event," as David C. Rubin highlights, "is telling a story" (11).

Representation or narration of memory in narrative fiction plays a significant role in the construction of individual characters' identity, the story worlds wherein they inhabit, and the narrative plots. From this perspective, literature is considered a lucrative source of memory-related theories since "literary fictions disseminate influential models of both individual and cultural memories as well as of the nature and functions of memory" (Neumann 333). "Memory and processes of remembering," in Bright Neumann's words, "have always been an important, indeed a dominant, topic in literature." Neumann draws our attention to the "Numerous texts [...] concerned with the mnemonic presence of the past in the present." Such texts, according to Neumann, "re-examine the relationship between the past and the present, and [...] illuminate the manifold functions that memories fulfill for the constitution of identity." The memory-oriented literary texts, as Neumann argues, "highlight that our memories are highly selective, and that the rendering of memories potentially tells us more about the rememberer's present, his or her desire and denial, than about the actual past events" (333). The narrators' mental states at the time of narration in *The Sea*, *The Gathering*, and *Milkman* act as the driving force of their storytelling activities through which they at least partially come to terms with their highly fictionalized past.

Memory is an indispensable part of human history. To put it in other words, "History," in Ilan Stavans's words, "is the living manifestation of memory, its theatre" (82). Memory played a significant role in ancient times, which functioned based on myths. Similarly, memory has been playing a meaningful role in modern times, which is mainly constructed based on science. In María Jesús Martínez-Alfaro's and Silvia Pellicer-Ortín's words:

> It is no wonder that Mnemosyne, the personification of memory in Greek mythology, should also be the mother of the Muses, inspiration to artists and poets and also goddesses of knowledge. A significant part of contemporary literature could be said to be presided by Mnemosyne, as many writers engage with the call to remember and to play aesthetically with memory and the frictions attending memory work. (15)

Accordingly, "the composition of a narrative text," as Stavans holds, "is a mnemonic act by the very fact that it involves *mneme* and *anamnesis*: it includes immediate and ancestral records, both innate and acquired" (emphasis original, 88). Thus, possibly it would not be wrong if one would claim that all narratives are about and/or are constructed by memories. In Charlotte Linde's words, "A narrative most typically is understood as a representation, or a construction, based on a sequence of events in the past, that communicates something from the memory of the narrator" (2).

Of all the three main types of memory in psychology — episodic, semantic (or propositional), and procedural — it is the first one, or "the memory of a specific personal event or a sequence of events" (Linde 2) which is usually presented in narrative. Being synonymous with autobiographical memory in Tulving's definition, "Episodic memory is concerned with unique, concrete, personal experiences dated in the rememberer's past" (*Elements* v). Remembering is an integral part of episodic memory, or in Tulving's words, "The basic unit of episodic memory is an individual act of remembering that begins with the witnessing or experiencing of an event or episode and ends with its subjective remembering (recollective experience)" (*Elements* 11). The three narratives analysed in this study primarily represent the individual processes of some experiential memories as they happened at particular times in the past. In other words, the stories we read are the result of the characters', narrators', recollectors', or storytellers', in Tulving's words, "subjective awareness of remembering" which is "One of the most compelling and salient characteristics of remembering of past events" (*Elements* 10).

It is Tulving's contention that humans are capable of mentally travelling back in time because of their sense of subjective time ("Episodic" 2). The subjective experience of memory is a primary narrative concern in *The Sea*, *The Gathering*, and *Milkman* where the presented narrative situations and events are based on the narrators' pure and conscious act of remembering and/or re-experiencing some specific events at particular times in the past. The narrators' acts of remembering are combinations of their recollections, retrievals and recalling. Since a complete retrieval is not possible, a full-scale replica of the original events is presented. Hence, the narrators' sense of identity is interwoven with their conscious narration of individual and collective memories. Through remembering, storying, and constructing memories, they endeavour to fill in some defining blank or confusing parts in their past lives. The void parts, to which they do not have direct access, include some fundamental information about their past lives.

"Storytelling," according to Astrid Erll, "is per definition an act of 'memory'" (213), and since "memory can only be reconstructed in time" (King 2), the first-person narrators in *The Sea*, *The Gathering*, and *Milkman* try to reconstruct their behaviour in the past through imagining some experienced personal events and retrospective narration of them. "The rediscovery of the past and its recreation in full detail," as Nicola King holds, "is a popular narrative trope" (65). "Memory and narration," in Andrea Smorti's words, "are both linked to the life and history of human culture" (19). The narrators' autobiographical memories also include "cultural-collective, often national" memories too (Erll 212). Hence, Smorti's argument about the similarities between narrative and autobiographical memory, which "[a]ccording to most definitions […] is the ability to consciously remember personal events" (Berntsen and Rubin "Understanding", 333), and which also holds true for the analysed narratives in this study. According to Smorti:

> Autobiographical memory and narrative are […] deeply interconnected and share common social roots. They are part of the second signal system, because both the memory of an event (in the form of an image, sound, voice, smell) and its narration through words are similar to signs or symbols that stand in place of the original object. In this way, they make the past in the present experienceable. (20)

Rather than considering "autobiographical memory as a subset of memory," Rubin underscores that "autobiographical memory is better considered as an expansion of memory" (5). Rubin also states that verbal narrative (words and/or stories), imagery and emotion are three main components of autobiographical memory (2-3). "Accuracy of memory" is also, as Rubin states, a "general issue" or "paradox" (4) in autobiographical memory. Furthermore, Rubin draws our attention to the constructed nature of autobiographical memories: "autobiographical memories are constructed. This does not mean that they are either accurate or inaccurate, but that they are not encoded, stored, and retrieved as wholes but rather are created at retrieval using components like the narrative, imagery, emotion division" (4). Thus, remembering has an experiential function in storytelling. Similarly, presentation of memory, according to Astrid Erll, plays a significant role in terms of the narrativity level in a single narrative. In other words, "it is in fictional representations of remembering that the manifold possibilities of narrative discourse best come to the fore" (213).

"Literature," according to Astrid Erll and Ansgar Nünning, "can virtually be described as a way to present individual memory" (282). In their essay, "Where literature and memory meet: towards a systematic approach to the concept of memory used in literary studies," Erll and Nünning discuss the nexus between memory and literature under three headings: The Memory of Literature, Memory in Literature, or Mimesis of Memory, and Literature as a Medium of Collective Memory. According to them, "Narrative texts in particular demonstrate forms that show a special affinity to memory" (282). They particularly highlight the function of memory in first-person narration:

> [I]t is not surprising that the narrative distinction between an experiencing and a narrating 'I' already rests on a (largely implicit) concept of memory: namely, on the concept of a difference between pre-narrative experience on the one hand, and on the other hand a memory which forms the past through narrative and retrospectively creates meaning. The occupation with first-person narrators is thus always an occupation with the literary presentation of memory. (282)

The mode of narration in the narratives analysed in this study is the first-person retrospective point of view. By adopting a superior perspective, the narrating I in each narrative recounts some painful/eventful traces of his/her memories to gain a deeper understanding of his/her experiencing I or self. Thus, the narrative construction in these narratives is based on the narrators' narrativization of the related memory. Their storytelling is heavily based on the operation of their consciousness. Likewise, Erll and Nünning consider the different processes of consciousness representation in narrative as "a further example of the ability of literature to represent memory, as it can bring conscious and unconscious processes of individual remembering to light through specifically fictional privileges" (282).

*The Sea*, *The Gathering*, and *Milkman* are mimeses of memory since the narrative acts represented in them are in fact memory practices. By considering "writing as a mnemonic act," Renate Lachmann argues that "When literature is considered in the light of memory, it appears as the mnemonic art par excellence. [… It is] culture's prominent (yet not only) representative of recording." In other words, "Writing," according to Lachmann, "is both an act of memory and a new interpretation, by which every new text is etched into memory space" (302). Likewise, "narrative," in Jens Brockmeier's words, "is crucial among [the] practices of memory" (26) as it "is capable of playing a number of different (cognitive, social and emotive) roles at the same time" (27). "[N]arrative's distinctive capacity," according to Brockmeier, is "to give shape to the temporal dimension of human experience" (27). Similarly, the narrators in the examined narratives try to make sense of their experiences by storying them. To do so, they recount their troubling autobiographical memories which, according to Alan Baddeley, refer "to the recollection by subjects of their earlier lives" (13) and are, in Dorthe Berntsen's and David C. Rubin's words, "crucial for a sense of identity, continuity, and direction in life" ("Introduction" 1). The narrators in these narratives are witnesses of a mostly forgotten order. Thus, they try to restore the painful order mainly in order to understand the nature of their own and the other characters' behaviour at that time. The main shared point in their stories is traumatic episodes. In other words, it is their open wounds that are bleeding the red ink into their autodiegetic narratives. However, the acts of recollection in their narratives mostly end in development, maturity, and self-awareness.

The line or border between fact and fiction, or imagination, is blurred in *The Sea*, *The Gathering*, and *Milkman*. To put the same idea in different words, the narrators' act of storytelling is a coproduction of their memories and imaginations. It helps them to defeat time and have a continuous sense of identity too. "Memory and imagination," in Kerry McSweeney's words, "collaborate to produce a narrative reconstruction of a life, in which individual episodes are seen to be parts of a continuum and the subject's continuity in time is shown" (93). The narrators' remembered memories are partly their (re)constructed memories too. Their remembering minds are the storehouses of what they remember, what they think they remember, and what they fabricate based on what they do not remember or what they have forgotten. They go through this process in order to define their identity at the time of narration. However, they do so based on their sense identity at the time of the remembered events. Accordingly, their memories are a constructive process through which they try to solidify and/or unify their identity via remembering and forgetting. Their memory is in line with Brady Wagoner's definition of the term, "Memory is not a thing, substance, or faculty for storing the representations of past but, rather, a process or activity of using the past to meet current needs for action" (5).

A remembering narrator is the most important element in the homodiegetic-autodiegetic narratives in *The Sea*, *The Gathering*, and *Milkman*. In other words, the first-person narrators are themselves the main participants in the events they narrate and are the protagonists in the storyworlds too. As self-conscious narrators and skilful storytellers, they try to (re)configure their personal histories.

Another shared property among these narratives is their similar focus on the representation of the autodiegetic narrators' memories. The long distance between the time of experience and the time of narration in all these narratives ease the evaluation process of the narrated events, for themselves and for the reader too. The three narrators are contemplators too in the sense that, while recounting their stories, they are meditating on the nature of their memories.

The triad of memory, identity, and time is the configuring structure based on which the narrators' acts of storytelling function. In their search for the truth and a personal sense of identity, remembering allows the narrators to defeat time by making a bond between their behaviour in the past and their evaluation of them in the present time. As a result of this process, they mostly come to terms with their experiences in the past. The fact that "Memory," as Nicola King holds, "can create the illusion of a momentary return to a lost past" (11) is also true about the primary point of remembering for the narrators. The interpretive nature of the narrators' remembering of the past takes place in terms of their present mentality. By "consisting more of holes than of bricks" (Albright 23), their remembered selves mostly remain an incomplete project. As Daniel Albright holds, "Literature is particularly suspicious of the remembered self" (21). Hence the represented remembered selves are entangled with a sense of oblivion, "The great writers are not only expert in memory; they are also expert in oblivion" (Albright 23). The remembered selves are, therefore, disorganized entities. As it is true about remembering in autobiographical narrative, memory "is only a metaphor, a dim surrogate for past time that can never be recovered, never embodied, never made to sit still" (Albright 39). The remembered selves in the examined narratives in the following three chapters are loose as they coincidentally include features from both the present and the absent or the present and past times. The narrators, however, try to achieve a unified and coherent sense of self or identity by the end of their acts of remembering.

Chapter Two analyses the two aspects of episodic memory in John Banville's *The Sea*. On the one hand, the narrator uses his act of remembering as a medium of his being and as an effective tool to fight against his mental and emotional problems. He feels lonely, detached and disappointed. Thus, he uses remembering as a remedy for his mental breakdown. As is argued, he uses storytelling to cure his melancholy as well as to examine the nature of remembering itself. While forgetting for him is synonymous with annihilation, remembering is equal with existing and being. Thus, as argued, memory in general and remembering in particular have ontological functions in *The Sea*. The narrator uses remembering as the only medium which connects him to some iconic events and people in his past life. However, his entire storytelling activity shows how remembering is always an incomplete act mixed with fabrication, construction, or imagination. Thus, it is the combination of the remembered or recounted memories with the constructed or fake ones which helps the narrator to come to terms with his past and to find some new possibilities for his life in the future.

In a similar way to the case in *The Sea*, remembering also, as Chapter Three argues, turns around a traumatic memory in Anne Enright's *The Gathering*. Enright's narrator scrutinizes her brother's suicidal death for the possible traces of what has brought about her own depression and mental breakdown. Since she does not have direct access to a great part of her and her family's past, she relies on her imagination so that she might find meaningful association among the apparently disconnected and irrelevant pieces. Despite the fact that she partially comes to terms with most of her life in the past with the help of her acts of remembering, this retrieving and constructing of memories fails to help her forgive Lamb Nugent for abusing her brother as the evilness of Nugent's actions extends beyond the scope of time in the past.

Reading Anna Burns's *Milkman* as a narrative of memory, Chapter Four studies the function of acts of remembering in this narrative. Unlike the shared concern and approach in *The Sea* and *The Gathering*, where the narrators' accounts are highly fictionalized, memory in *Milkman* is represented as a reliable tool which faithfully registers personal and socio-cultural histories and realities. Thus, remembering in *Milkman* provides the narrator with an opportunity for re-experiencing a painful period in her life in the past. With her mature perspective, she narrates in order to evaluate and interpret her own behaviour during the Troubles on the one hand and to understand both her younger self and those around her in the past on the other hand. Establishing her distinctive sense of identity and identifying her strategies to survive the deadly threats of a problematic society are the two main payoffs of the narrator's acts of remembering and storytelling activity in *Milkman*.

The narrators in *The Sea* and *The Gathering* are writers, and in *Milkman*, a storyteller. All three narrators are experienced, knowledgeable, and conscious characters who try to go beyond their disturbing memories. Their pasts are made up of fragmented pieces of memories. By narrating them, the narrators try to organize their memories because, as Smorti says, "memory becomes more and more structured in a narrative way" (70), and "Creating stories plays an irreplaceable role in understanding oneself" (119). Thus, the narrativization of the narrators' memories on the one hand facilitates their understanding of some fundamental issues in their past; on the other hand, it helps them to fill the voids in their memories through storying them. In other words, whenever the narrators' memories fail to provide them with first-hand access to the past events and/or situations, they use their storytelling skill to construct a related memory which makes the truth accessible to them. The construction of memory plays an important role in the narrators' understanding and acceptance of the past. Thus, their identity or selfhood is constructed through remembering and representing their memories. However, their *anamnesis*[4] fails to end in their desired truths regarding their self-identity. In other words, in the examined narratives, travelling in time through remembering does not end in divine revelation and/or relief.

Having analysed the issue of memory in Eliot's, Proust's and Woolf's works and by drawing on Freud's essay "On Transience," Evelyne Ender draws her conclusion that "the memory garden is our subjective creation; our imagination, desire, and affections determine the salience, significance, and beauty we ascribe to chosen elements of the surrounding world. As the culmination of these different aesthetic and psychological impulses, autobiographical memory becomes our bulwark against the forces of destruction and mortality" (179-180). Likewise, the narrators in the three examined narratives rely on their episodic or experiential memories as shields against their mental complications. They are both recounting and performing their acts of remembering. Through their storytelling activities, the narrators try to re-experience some iconic events in

---

[4] According to Jens Brockmeier, "For Plato [...] the notion of anamnesis (recollection) implied that memory is the golden path to the highest intellectual and spiritual truths a human being could know. True recall could lead one's soul back to its origin, to that divine state of knowledge and being one had experienced before birth. Those unable to recollect what they had known prior to drinking of the waters of Lethe (forgetfulness) were condemned to live out their lives in the shadowy world of the mundane without ever reaching any insight into their fundamentally spiritual and divine nature" (16).

their past lives so that they can counter their negative effects, such as disappointments and depression, at the time of narration; so that they can reframe their identities. As argued in the next chapter, the narrator's acts of remembering in *The Sea* help him to reframe his negative thoughts about some troubling episodes from his life in the past.

# TWO
# Shadow of the Past: Narration and the Creation of Memory in John Banville's *The Sea*

> "The past beats inside me like a second heart."
> (Banville 13)

John Banville (1945- ) is a Booker and Franz Kafka prize-winning contemporary Irish author. Banville's art of writing shares the main features of Irish literary writing. In Eva Patten's words, "Metafictional and philosophical writing in Ireland continues to be dominated, however, by John Banville. Since the mid-1980s, Banville's fiction has continued its analysis of alternative languages and structures of perception" (272). Banville's work, according to Mark O'Connell, "is endlessly concerned with the divisions and confusions between components of experience: self and world, truth and falsehood, memory and imagination. One such endlessly scrutinised dichotomy is that between the out-turned and the in-turned halves of the self" (91). Likewise, the whole structure of narrative plot as well as content turns around the representation of these two aspects of experience in Banville's thirteenth novel *The Sea*, where the narrator's subjective remembering is the primary focus of his autobiographical narration. However, Banville in his novel does not present recollection as a straightforward mental activity since, mixed with imagination, memory has an elusive and/or evasive nature, and as a result the narrator's sense of identity is uncertain and undergoing a constant process of (re)construction.

With *The Sea*, as Neil Murphy rightly argues, "Banville attained a level of technical achievement beyond anything he had previously managed, creating a fluent interdependency of the novel's myriad components (temporal, ontological, intertextual)" (328-329). However, according to Murphy's argument, the narrative shares some of the "classical Banvillean preoccupations," — "The self-reflexive observations about the limits of language, the treachery of memory, and the hazards of locating a fixed version of truth" (322). By stating that "The role of trauma has played a relatively minor role in critical approaches to this text [*The Sea*]," Kathleen Costello-Sullivan highlights the element of trauma in Banville's narrative by holding that "*The Sea* arguably provides the most comprehensive portrait of traumatic loss in Banville's canon" (*Trauma* 34).

Finding himself on a "Lost track" (Banville 218), the narrator in *The Sea* holds to his episodic memories in order to overcome his confusion. Although he is aware that it is mixed with "fancy" (Banville 243), memory for Max Morden has the capacity to represent the truth since it "dislikes motion, preferring to hold things still" (Banville 221). The series of acts of remembering begin with the grown-up narrator's physical return to the site of his childhood holidays. This event triggers his long recollecting process which brings about *The Sea*'s narrative since, as he admits, "one might almost live one's life over, if only one could make a sufficient effort of recollection" (Banville 160).

Thus, *The Sea* is a narrative primarily about the narrator's memory of the past events and their impact on his sense of identity. In Caren McCarthy's words, "Banville [in *The Sea*] sets his protagonist the impossible task of re-presenting or re-inhabiting the past" (165). The narrator's acts of storytelling and remembering are the devices through which he consciously tries to do the impossible task, "There are moments when the past has a force so strong it seems one might be annihilated by it" (Banville 47). Memory in *The Sea* is used as a medium for retrieving the narrator's painful experiences. "[T]he focus on memory," in Derek Hand's words, "is one more way to re-engage with the past on a personal level, to reopen it and examine it for the present moment" (31).

The first-person narrator in *The Sea* is continuously haunted by some of his specific experiences—with his own parents when he was a child, with a family called the Graces when he was twelve years old, with his recently deceased wife, and with his daughter. Not being able to "Stop thinking" (Banville 186) about his past life, the narrator is "tired," with an "unsettling" mind (Banville 184 and 186) which sometimes "just empties" (Banville 244). Beyond all his out-turned mental concerns, his autobiographical narration has a selfward intention. In his fifties, he tries to understand his own life and identity. He hopes to define and/or find his own sense of identity in all his remarkable experiences through his recollections. In other words, as a historian himself, Max writes the story of his own life so that he can understand himself and others. In this sense, he is a typical Banvillian character, "Banville's main characters strive to write or tell their stories, in order to find a meaning for their existence in relation to the others and the world and they are all isolated in their effort, [...] The traditional narrative quest transforms itself into a critical narrative of self-questioning" (Fiorato 61). The repeating (un)conscious question in Max's mind is whether his knowledge of and/or attention to the others has helped him to know himself.

Memory, however, is presented as a fraud, unstable, and thus unreliable mental aspects and capacities come to the fore in *The Sea*, where narration of memory is as important as the creation and construction of it. Based on the shadows of some memories, Max Morden is remembering and at the same time as pretending to remember some episodes from his past. Thus, his storytelling is about memory and also, in his own words, "Memory's prodigious memory" (Banville 161). Wherever possible, he consciously plays with this aspect of memory. For example, when he fails to retrieve the memory of kissing his young adolescent girlfriend Chloe on the day they went to the picture house, he makes fun of memory, "Really, Madam Memory, I take back all my praise, if it is Memory herself who is at work here and not some other, more fanciful muse" (Banville 163). Such moments in his narrative show the high degree of his conscious act of remembering, and illustrate the fact that memory is insufficient to replace reality.

Similarly, the blurring distinction between the two versions of the narrator's I—in the past and present times—is presented as a main cause of Max Morden's identity problem in *The Sea*. The remembering self is presented as a disorganized and disintegrated entity. Through reviewing his memories, he falls into an existential hole. Thus, the narrative plot in *The Sea* is constructed out of memory patches of different times brought together by a memory-narrating and memory-constructing narrator. The weaving function of memory gives the narrative its overall cohesion and integration. The narrator has a past full of traumatic events. His desire to talk about his personal life is out of his mental need. He recounts his autobiography in order to alleviate his suffering.

Parallel narrative technique is a defining tool of narration in *The Sea*. Without any meaningful order, the narrator simultaneously and in the manner of stream of consciousness recounts and follows some storylines from different times — his stay in the Cedars at the time of narration; his experience with the Graces half a century ago; his life with his wife Anna and her illness and untimely death; and his relationship with his mother and daughter. The circular nature of time in his narration allows the narrator to expose the ruling impact of past in his life. Acts of remembering are presented as an annihilating device of time in *The Sea*. His constant sense of identity, however, is presented as independent from the flow of time, "The truth is, it has all begun to run together, past and possible future and impossible present" (Banville 96).

Although Max Morden's "memory gropes in search of details, solid objects, the components of the past" (Banville 87), his remembering process is selective or episodic as his storytelling is based on what he remembers. When he does not or cannot retrieve a memory, he does not dwell on it. Rather, he only retells the facts and moves on to the next memory. For example, when he finds out that he does not "recall under what circumstances exactly [he] managed eventually to get inside the Cedars" (Banville 85), he does not linger on the memory. Similarly, some episodes, or memory patches, are quite clear in his mind, "There is a multicoloured patch in my memory of the moment, a shimmer of variegated brightness where her [] hands hover" (Banville 86).

*The Sea* has two parts. Part I (pp. 3-132) begins with the narrator's visit to a house called the Cedars in a little seaside village, where he would go with his family in summers when he was twelve years old. His staying in the place opens his old wounds. Part I mainly covers the narrator's acquaintance with the Graces who are the primary concern in his acts of remembering. He begins his remembering with his memory of the family's children to whom he refers as the Gods and with whom he had his first experience of desire. The main narrative point is presented in the first line, "THEY DEPARTED, the gods" (emphasis original, 3). Hence the narrative presents its main theme at its onset. The narrator's desire to re-experience the life he had before the gods' departing drives the progression of the entire narrative. Nearly all the embedded narratives presented in part I also continue in part II (pp. 135-262). The focus in part II, however, is the endings — the death of the Grace twins, his wife's death, and his return home.

## 2.1 The Ontological Functions of Remembering

The narrator in *The Sea* defines himself as "a little vessel of sadness [...] sailing in this muffled silence through the autumn dark" (Banville 72). The medium of his sailing is his storytelling which happens in the uncertain realm of his memory. Most of the qualities of his narrative are highlighted in his characterization of himself as "a person of scant talent and scanter ambition, greyed o'er by the years, uncertain and astray and in need of consolation and the brief respite of drink-induced oblivion" (Banville 200). The narrator relies on his memory to investigate his own identity and relationships.

Memory in *The Sea* is presented as a medium of contemplation. Max Morden's acts of remembering, through triggering his emotional and cognitive reactions to past events, provide him with situations based on which he has a phenomenological and ontological subjective experience. Not only is he concerned with the nature of identity and consciousness, but he also scrutinizes his unique place among his relationships. In other words, he tries to find out what knowing himself and others means and how he can do so, "The question I am left with now, anyway, is precisely the question of knowing" (Banville 217). His acts of remembering are, thus, mainly at the service of his philosophical mind which, in his own words, is concerned with "Fruitless interrogation" (Banville 218).

*The Sea* is presented as the narrator's cognitive journey which is intended to bring about a cure for him through examining some formative moments in his past, "These days I must take the world in small and carefully measured doses, it is a sort of homeopathic cure I am undergoing, though I am not certain what this cure is meant to mend. Perhaps I am learning to live amongst the living again. Practising, I mean. But no, that is not it. Being here is just a way of not being anywhere" (Banville 192). At the time of narration, the narrator has fallen "into a mood of bitter melancholy" (Banville 252).

The fact that Max Morden is losing the power of his memory is frightening to him. He feels as if he is "wandering through the chamber of horrors" in his "head" (Banville 212). His remembering, thus, is his fight against his semi dementia: "There are times, they occur with increasing frequency nowadays, when I seem to know nothing, when everything I did know seems to have fallen out of my mind like a shower of rain, and I am gripped for a moment in paralysed dismay, waiting for it all to come back but with no certainty that it will" (Banville 212). His act of remembering is an intentional act of bringing back his memories so that he can continuously maintain a coherent sense of identity.

Max Morden's autobiographical narration not only includes some episodic memories from his past life from different times, but also his narration relates to his contemplation of the nature of memory. His storytelling is, thus, an attempt to find persuasive answers to some of his identity-related questions. For example, in the following passage, the narrator compares his two selves, the old and the new: "How is it that in childhood everything new that caught my interest had an aura of the uncanny, since according to all the authorities the uncanny is not some new thing but a thing known re-turning in a different form, become a revenant? So many unanswerables, this the least of them" (Banville 10). Similarly, he compares his life at the time of narration with the one at the time of the recollected story, "So much of life was stillness then, when we were young, or so it seems now; a biding stillness; a vigilance" (Banville 12). He presents his experienced adult mind as capable of discerning the states of his younger self. For example, when he arrives in the Cedars, the atmosphere of his younger self returns:

> When we arrived, I marvelled to see how much of the village as I remembered it was still here, if only for eyes that knew where to look, mine, that is. It was like encountering an old flame behind whose features thickened by age the slender lineaments that a former self so loved can still be clearly discerned. (Banville 46-47)

In exploring his life at two different times, the narrator's mind experiences oscillation between two times and two different mental states—the imagined and the reported. The narrator's conscious detachment from his two selves allows him to have an objective narration as much as possible. For example, in one scene he imagines himself and the twins, Chloe and Myles, from the perspective of a third self, "What phantom version of me is it that watches us—them—those three children—as they grow indistinct in that cinereal air and then are gone through the gap that will bring them out at the foot of Station Road? (Banville 137). In his narration, he highlights the continuous nature of his identity despite the physical changes he has had through time. He is completely transported to the emotional and subjective world of his childhood when he stands at the Cedars: "Now here I was at the farm gate again, the child of those days grown corpulent and half-grey and almost old" (Banville 53).

Max Morden is aware of the uncontrollable nature of his mind or mental functioning: "I cannot stop. How wild the unguarded fancy runs" (Banville 201). In his adult life, he is mentally engaged in his experiences: "My mind balked in its calculations like a confused and weary old beast of burden" (Banville 56). The associating nature of his memories and the continuity and connectivity of the past and present times are all the results of the operational manner of his philosophical, wandering mind. He cannot focus on his memories since his minds wanders off: "How the mind wanders, even on the most concentrated of occasions" (Banville 15).

Max Morden's acts of remembering are closely related to his identity. His entire narrative provides us with a map of his sense of identity through time:

> From earliest days I wanted to be someone else. The injunction *nosce te ipsum* had an ashen taste on my tongue from the first time a teacher enjoined me to repeat it after him. I knew myself, all too well, and did not like what I

> knew. Again, I must qualify. It was not what I was that I disliked, I mean the singular, essential me—although I grant that even the notion of an essential, singular self is problematic—but the congeries of affects, inclinations, received ideas, class tics, that my birth and upbringing had bestowed on me in place of a personality. In place of, yes. I never had a personality, not in the way that others have, or think they have. I was always a distinct no-one, whose fiercest wish was to be an indistinct someone. I know what I mean. (Banville 216)

His acts of remembering his experiences with Chloe and Anna reveal their impact on his identity and the formation of "an indistinct someone" (Banville 216) at the core of his personality through time. Inwardly, he achieves an established and satisfying sense of identity via Anna, his recently deceased wife. His remembering is a reaction to the shattering of that acquired integrity by her death.

Max Morden narrates in order to tell himself and us about his true identity—how he has become who he is. To do so, he sets out from a historic event that happened in his life at the early stages of his adolescence when all of a sudden, he experienced a change in his sense of identity as a result of being introduced into the circle of the Graces: "I was myself and at the same time someone else, someone completely other, completely new" (Banville 145). In his narrative of the Graces, he wonders how he defined himself and his identity through them: "How proud I was to be seen with them, these divinities, for I thought of course that they were the gods, so different were they from anyone I had hitherto known" (Banville 108). Similarly, he acknowledges his personal intention of using the Graces as a social ladder to recreate his personal identity apart from his highly stratified society: "The social structure of our summer world was as fixed and hard of climbing as a ziggurat. [...] That I had managed to scramble from the base of those steep social steps all the way up to the level of the Graces seemed, like my secret passion for Connie Grace, a token of specialness, of being the one chosen among so many of the unelect. The gods had singled me out for their favour" (Banville 109). In his comment on the experience, he acknowledges his own class-consciousness as the main factor in his relationship with the Graces: "I will not deny it, I was always ashamed of my origins, ... [my] indignation and hot resentment. From the start I was bent on bettering myself. What was it that I wanted from Chloe Grace but to be on the level of her family's superior social position, however briefly, at whatever remove?" (Banville 207).

Max Morden's long stage of fantasising the Graces comes to an end when, during "a timeless minute or two," he experiences an authentic event for the first time in his life: "suddenly I was allowed to see under her skirt along the inner side of her thigh all the way up to the hollow of her lap and the plump mound there sheathed in tensed white cotton. […]. I stared and stared, my brow growing hot and my palms wet" (Banville 117). Having witnessed Mrs. Grace's private self, he immediately feels a "a sour sense of deflation […] puzzled, and strangely resentful, too, as if I were the one, not she, whose private self had been intruded upon and abused. It was a manifestation of the goddess I had witnessed, no doubt of that, but the instant of divinity had been disconcertingly brief" (Banville 117-118). Max Morden presents this memory as a rite of passage in his life by showing how it helped him see the real, rather than the symbolic, woman:

> Under my greedy gaze Mrs. Grace had been transformed from woman into demon and then in a moment was mere woman again. One moment she was Connie Grace, her husband's wife, her children's mother, the next she was an object of helpless veneration, a faceless idol, ancient and elemental, conjured by the force of my desire, and then something in her had suddenly gone slack, and I had felt a qualm of revulsion and shame, not shame for myself and what I had purloined of her but, obscurely, for the woman herself, and not for anything she had done, either, but for what she was, as with a hoarse moan she turned on her side and toppled into sleep, no longer a demon temptress but herself only, a mortal woman. (Banville 118)

His memory of Mrs. Grace primarily reveals the impact of his unique experience on his young mind. He undergoes a cognitive transformation when, as a result of his "greedy gaze," he sees the reality of female body in Mrs. Grace. This knowledge curbs his strong desire: "I glanced at Mrs. Grace asleep, glanced almost with contempt. All at once she was no more than a big archaic lifeless torso, the felled effigy of some goddess no longer worshipped by the tribe and thrown out on the midden, a target for the village boys with their slingshots and their bows and arrows" (Banville 124).

Similarly, his sexual desire for Mrs. Grace has transformed through time. In his remembering how he felt towards her in the past in "a series of vivid tableaux" (Banville 125), he highlights the change: "I have not been so close to a grown-up woman since I was a child in my mother's arms, but in place of desire now I feel only a kind of surly dread" (Banville 126).

Max Morden's acts of remembering present the (trans)formational process of his sense of identity through his life. In his narration, he highlights the impact of his first experience of love as well as his marriage on his ontological formation throughout the years. Although from different perspectives, the two events evenly contribute to the establishment of his sense of identity. Describing her as "the Sphinx" and himself as one of her "priests" (Banville 237), he recounts his love of Chloe "as if I were carrying within me a phial of the most precious and delicately combustible material" (Banville 167). He shares with us the reasons Chloe's character, behaviour, and complicated approach to him still haunt the main part of his consciousness:

> [T]hose weeks with Chloe were for me a series of more or less enraptured humiliations. She accepted me as a suppliant at her shrine with disconcerting complacency. In her more distracted moods, she would hardly deign to notice my presence, and even when she gave me her fullest attention there was always a flaw in it, a fleck of preoccupation, of absence. This wilful vagueness tormented and infuriated me, but worse was the possibility that it might not be willed. That she might choose to disdain me I could accept, could welcome, even, in an obscurely pleasurable way, but the thought that there were intervals when I simply faded to transparency in her gaze, no, that was not to be borne. (Banville 164)

As a reaction to Chloe's challenging character, Max Morden is still looking for some persuasive reasons in his examination of the nature of his own reaction towards her complicated behaviour and why, despite her constant humiliations, he insisted on what he describes as protecting her. His comments in this case reveal his solipsism and the fact that how, more than functioning based on realities, his mental functioning at that time was under the spell of possibility and plausibility. Admiring his own "tactfulness," Max Morden tells us, he reminds himself of the reasons he "put up with her [Chloe's] caprices" and "high-handedness" (Banville 165):

> My forbearance in Chloe's case was due, I believe, to a strong urge of protectiveness that I had toward her. [...] Since she was the one on whom I had chosen, or had been chosen, to lavish my love, she must be preserved as nearly flawless as possible, spiritually and in her actions. It was imperative that I save her from herself and her faults. The task fell to me naturally since her faults were her faults, and she could not be expected to evade their bad effects by her own volition. And not only must she be saved from these faults and their consequences for her behaviour but she must be kept from all knowledge of them, too, in so far as it was possible for me to do so. And not just her active faults. Ignorance, incapacity of insight, dull complacency, such things too must be masked, their manifestations denied. The fact for instance that she did not know that she was later in my affections than her mother, of all people, made her seem almost piteously vulnerable in my eyes. Mark, the issue was not the fact of her being a late-comer in my affections, but her ignorance of that fact. If she were somehow to find out my secret she would likely be let down in her own estimation, would think herself a fool not to have seen what I felt for her mother, and might even be tempted to feel second to her mother in having been my second choice. And that must not be. (Banville 165-166)

Max's care for Chloe's unique character stemmed from his perception that she mirrored his character and thoughts. In other words, his intention was to protect himself through recognizing her uniqueness. He did so by keeping the truth away from her and enduring the ultimate humiliation on her part. For example, he was careful to have "no confrontations, no brutal enlightenments, no telling of terrible truths. [...] I must not tell her that I had loved her mother before I loved her, that she smelled of stale biscuits, or that Joe from the Field had remarked the green tinge of her teeth" (Banville 167). Besides through hiding the truth, he protected her through mirroring his own character into hers: "Her self-esteem was of far less importance to me than my own, although the latter was dependent on the former. If her sense of herself were tainted, by doubt or feelings of foolishness or of lack of perspicacity, my regard for her would itself be tainted" (Banville 167). As a result of her disruptive behaviour and complex character, he experiences a big change and difference in his short life for the first time:, "In her I had my first experience of the absolute otherness of other people.

[...] in Chloe the world was first manifest for me as an objective entity. [...] no one had yet been real in the way that Chloe was. And if she was real, so, suddenly, was I. She was I believe the true origin in me of self-consciousness. Before, there had been one thing and I was part of it, now there was me and all that was not me" (Banville 167-168). He describes her as if she transplanted him into an exotic world:

> In severing me from the world and making me realise myself in being thus severed, she expelled me from that sense of the immanence of all things, the all things that had included me, in which up to then I had dwelt, in more or less blissful ignorance. Before, I had been housed, now I was in the open, in the clearing, with no shelter in sight. I did not know that I would not get inside again, through that ever straitening gate. (Banville 168)

Chloe's impact on Max Morden's perception of himself and of others outlives their short encounter. Later when he meets Anna and marries her, recognition of the otherness of each other plays the most significant role in their relationship, "The philosophers tell us that we are defined and have our being through others. [...] Who was to know me, if not Anna? Who was to know Anna, if not I? Absurd questions" (Banville 217). He presents Anna as a character who forged his identity by letting him develop his own true self: "What Anna proposed to me, [...] was not so much marriage as the chance to fulfil the fantasy of myself" (Banville 105). Telling his memories of her emboldens him to stick to the core of his established identity. Decades after his infatuation with Chloe for abstract and fanciful reasons, Max finds his true identity in Anna.

Describing Anna as "being the product of a classless class" (Banville 208), Max Morden describe her as a person who let him be, not become, who he really was. His storytelling is his mourning for her recent death after which he finds himself alone, lonely, and unprotected: "how could you go and leave me like this, floundering in my own foulness, with no one to save me from myself. How could you" (Banville 196). As it is the main goal of his act of remembering, Max Morden tries to keep her memories fresh by constantly imagining her. He is worried about forgetting her: "I was thinking of Anna. I make myself think of her, I do it as an exercise. She is lodged in me like a knife and yet I am beginning to forget her. Already the image of her that I hold in my head is fraying, bits of pigments, flakes of gold leaf, are chipping off. Will the entire canvas be empty one day?" (Banville 215) Storying his memories with Anna has an ultimate personal goal—knowing himself through his experiences. Through recounting what he remembers, he intends to know the dark corners of his self in the past and the present. He does so by evaluating the people in his life via his memories:

> I have come to realize how little I knew her, I mean how shallowly I knew her, how ineptly. I do not blame myself for this. Perhaps I should. Was I too lazy, too inattentive, too self-absorbed? Yes, all of those things, and yet I cannot think it is a matter of blame, this forgetting, this not-having-known. I fancy, rather, that I expected too much, in the way of knowing. I know so little of myself, how should I think to know another? (Banville 215)

Thus, the narrator in *The Sea* tries to mend his ontological insecurity through his storytelling which is in one sense his desperate effort to know the people who have influenced his life deeply. In his narrative, he simulates how he felt and what he thought about his relationship with Anna:

> The truth is, we did not wish to know each other. More, what we wished was exactly that, not to know each other. […] that what I found in Anna from the first was a way of fulfilling the fantasy of myself. I did not know quite what I meant when I said it, but thinking now on it a little I suddenly see. Or do I. Let me try to tease it out, I have plenty of time, these Sunday evenings are endless. (Banville 215-216)

Max Morden's narrative illustrates his journey from outward concerns towards inward ones following his experience with Chloe. His finds out that his infatuation with Anna was not because of her selfish character and humiliating approach towards him; rather, it was because she recognized his true identity and let him be whoever he was. By doing this, she became "the medium of [his] transmutation" (Banville 216). The metamorphosis he highlights in the following passage refers to the replacement of his desire to be somebody with his longing to be nobody:

> She was the fairground mirror in which all my distortions would be made straight. "Why not be yourself?" she would say to me in our early days together—be, mark you, not know—[...] Be yourself! Meaning, of course, Be anyone you like. That was the pact we made, that we would relieve each other of the burden of being the people whom everyone else told us we were. Or at least she relieved me of that burden, but what did I do for her? Perhaps I should not include her in this drive toward unknowing, perhaps it was only I who desired ignorance. (Banville 216-217)

Max Morden's embedded narrative of Anna has a central place in *The Sea*. It is the conclusion by which his autobiographical narrative comes to end. Towards the end, his storytelling changes into a practice of remembering Anna. He is frightened by forgetting her: "Why have you (Anna) not come back to haunt me? It is the least I would have expected of you. Why this silence day after day, night after interminable night? It is like a fog, this silence of yours" (Banville 247). In her absence, his judgment of their relationship reveals his perspective towards the capacity of his work as an artist: "Why should I demand more veracity of vision of myself than of a great and tragic artist?" (Banville 218) Similarly, he finds out that with his acts of remembering he cannot fill in some deep holes in his past life and relationships: "Why do I torment myself with these insoluble equivocations, have I not had enough of casuistry?" (Banville 218). By describing the result of his long storytelling process as a fallacy, Max Morden concludes that his storytelling based on remembering some episodes from the past events is insufficient to fill the ontological void he has been finding himself in recently. Acts of remembering, in other words, fail to end his feeling of ontological insecurity.

## 2.2 Max Morden's Struggle with his Fading Memory

Memory in *The Sea* is presented as an integral part of consciousness. Moreover, it is an abstract and fabricated entity. Relativism and adaptability are presented as its main qualities. "[M]emories," in the narrator's words, "are always eager to match themselves seamlessly to the things and places of a revisited past" (Banville 148). As it is for us, the past for the experienced writer-narrator in *The Sea* is a fictional world in which some episodes from his experiences are "held suspended" (Banville 246). Of other experiences, he has "only jagged and ill-lit flickers of recollection" (Banville 253). Thus, in his recollection, the narrator toils to find some invisible and irretrievable pieces of his life in the past as he "cannot rid [himself] of the conviction that [… he] missed something", although he does not "know what it might have been" (Banville 218).

Max Morden's act of remembering is a conscious mental activity. Comparing himself to an artist, he paints his past life through delineating the "central figures [in his life] …. on the wall of [his] memory." However, apart from Rose's "completed portrait" in his recollections, the portraits of the other characters such as Chloe and her mother, are "blurred" (Banville 223 and 224). His memory book resembles "a Book of the Dead," a "miniature," "a sort of cameo" (Banville 237 and 243). He is aware of his acts of misremembering. For example, when he talks about a man who came to his side at the beach, he knowingly recounts what he imagines as well as what he invents, "The shoes I may have invented" (Banville 245).

The narrator's autobiographical narration is framed by some iconic episodes from his past life not because of his intentional choice, but as a result of his fading memory. Since both in his own words, "Live in the past, do I" (Banville 69), and in the words of his daughter, ""You live in the past"" (Banville 60), he has "nothing of any originality to say" (Banville 40) other than his fragmented memories. In his own analogy, his act of storytelling is similar to putting on the past. In revisiting his childhood place, he feels "nervous […] the moment when I would have to take on the house, to put it on, as it were, like something I had worn in another, prelapsarian life, a once fashionable hat, say, an outmoded pair of shoes, or a wedding suit, smelling of mothballs and no longer fitting around the waist and too tight under the arms but bulging with memories in every pocket" (Banville 155-156).

Although Max Morden's "memory gropes in search of details, solid objects, the components of the past" (Banville 87), his remembering is selective, and his storytelling is based on what he remembers and what he pretends to. Therefore, the plot in *The Sea* turns around the vividness of some episodes as much as the vagueness of the other ones. For example, not only can the narrator remember some defining moments from his wife Anna, but he can also imagine her clearly: "her wild smell in my nostrils and the heat of her hair against my cheek" (Banville 105). In other words, some episodes, or memory patches, are quite clear in his mind: "There is a multicoloured patch in my memory of the moment, a shimmer of variegated brightness where her [...] hands hover" (Banville 86). However, he cannot retrieve some of his memories which are important in his reconstruction of the past. For example, he does not "recall under what circumstances exactly [he] managed eventually to get inside the Cedars" (Banville 85). Similarly, in imagining his relationship with Chloe, he admits, "I do recall a kiss, one out of the so many that I have forgotten" (Banville 141). He does not hesitate regarding what he does not or cannot remember. He only acknowledges his facts and moves forward in the chain of his memories.

However, despite the fact that he has lost most of his memories through time, his adult subjectivity is functioning based on some solid memories. For example, he vividly remembers a scene from his childhood: "I have carried the memory of that moment through a whole half century, as if it were the emblem of something final, precious and irretrievable" (Banville 159-160). Thus, the real world for him is the cosy world of the past which is the centre of his life too:

> [W]hen I look back I see that the greater part of my energies was always given over to the simple search for shelter, for comfort, for, yes, I admit it, for cosiness. This is a surprising, not to say a shocking, realisation. Before, I saw myself as something of a buccaneer, facing all-comers with a cutlass in my teeth, but now I am compelled to acknowledge that this was a delusion. To be concealed, protected, guarded, that is all I have ever truly wanted, to burrow down into a place of womby warmth and cower there, hidden from the sky's indifferent gaze and the harsh air's damagings. That is why the past is just such a retreat for me, I go there eagerly, rubbing my hands and shaking off the cold present and the colder future. And yet, what existence, really, does it have, the past? After all, it is only what the present was, once, the present that is gone, no more than that. And yet. (Banville 60-61)

Whenever needed and necessary, Max Morden reconfigures his memory system in order to make up a whole meaning out of his life. Memory is the ultimate reality for him. For example, at the end of sharing his memory of Mrs. Grace, he highlights the centrality and superiority of remembering as immortality:

> She is in my memory her own avatar. Which is the more real, the woman reclining on the grassy bank of my recollections, or the strew of dust and dried marrow that is all the earth any longer retains of her? No doubt for others elsewhere she persists, a moving figure in the wax-works of memory, but their version will be different from mine, and from each other's. Thus in the minds of the many does the one ramify and disperse. It does not last, it cannot, it is not immortality. (Banville 118-119)

He considers remembering as the ultimate truth beyond which there is nothing. In other words, remembering is his religion:

> We carry the dead with us only until we die too, and then it is we who are borne along for a little while, and then our bearers in their turn drop, and so on into the unimaginable generations. I remember Anna, our daughter Claire will remember Anna and remember me, then Claire will be gone and there will be those who remember her but not us, and that will be our final dissolution. True, there will be something of us that will remain, a fading photograph, a lock of hair, a few fingerprints, a sprinkling of atoms in the air of the room where we breathed our last, yet none of this will be us, what we are and were, but only the dust of the dead. (Banville 119)

Max Morden's memory structure, therefore, is dynamic by virtue of being continuously under (re)construction. It is an ongoing process throughout the narrative. In his failure to "catch up with" the complete features of his adolescent-period sweetheart Chloe Grace, he calls our attention to the manner of his act of remembering by highlighting its incomplete, yet at the same time unavoidable, quality, "All this I remember, intensely remember, yet it is all disparate, I cannot assemble it into a unity. Try as I may, pretend as I may, I am unable to conjure her […] I cannot, in short, see her. She wavers before my memory's eye at a fixed distance, always just beyond focus, moving backward at exactly the same rate as I am moving forward" (Banville 139). Max Morden finds it baffling that people might exist independently from being remembered and or imagined: "Once out of my presence she should by right become pure figment, a memory of mine, a dream of mine, but all the evidence told me that even away from me she remained solidly, stubbornly, incomprehensibly herself. And yet people do go, do vanish. That is the greater mystery; the greatest. I too could go, oh, yes, at a moment's notice I could go and be as though I had not been" (Banville 140).

The narrativized past is a combination of real and unreal elements. It is an act of representation as well as pretention. Despite that, the past is the only place where the narrator desires to be: "The past, I mean the real past, matters less than we pretend. [...] I had been travelling for a long time, for years, and had at last arrived at the destination to where, all along, without knowing it, I had been bound, and where I must stay, it being, for now, the only possible place, the only possible refuge, for me" (Banville 157). The mixed nature of memory, or its real and unreal aspects, in *The Sea* is obvious from the opening lines which reveal the narrator's intentional act of remembering his past life through the involuntary impact of his dreams. Seemingly, he finds himself at a home, at the Cedars, where he experienced what has been lingering with him throughout all his life: "A dream it was that drew me here [...] I was determinedly on my way somewhere, going home, it seemed, although I did not know what or where exactly home might be" (Banville 24). His dreams are awakening as they cue the latent emotions in his mind: "Immediately then [...] I thought of Ballyless and the house there on Station Road, and the Graces, and Chloe Grace, I cannot think why, and it was as if I had stepped suddenly out of the dark into a splash of pale, salt-washed sunlight. It endured only a minute, less than a minute, that happy lightsomeness, but it told me what to do, and where I must go" (Banville 26). Thus encouraged by his dreams, Max Morden is transported to his memory world the time of which is interwoven with the time of remembering. When he opens the gate of the Cedars, the creak of the door vibrates memory of the experience he had there in the past: "They creak, this present gate, that past sign, to this day, to this night, in my dreams" (Banville 13). The integration of past and present is thus at the core in his narration of his memories.

Imagination of the past for the narrator is at first similar to its reincarnation. The freshness of memory is appalling to him at the beginning: "I am amazed at how little has changed in the more than fifty years that have gone by since I was last here. Amazed, and disappointed, I would go so far as to say appalled, for reasons that are obscure to me, since why should I desire change, I who have come back to live amidst the rubble of the past?" (Banville 4) For example, he vividly remembers the details of the first time he met Mr Grace:

> I had paused by the gate, frankly eavesdropping, and now suddenly a man with a drink in his hand came out of the house. He was short and top-heavy, all shoulders and chest and big round head, with close-cut, crinkled, glittering-black hair with flecks of premature grey in it and a pointed black beard likewise flecked. He wore a loose green shirt unbuttoned and khaki shorts and was barefoot. His skin was so deeply tanned by the sun it had a purplish sheen. Even his feet, I noticed, were brown on the insteps. (Banville 6)

Max Morden in this passage recounts his memory of the first impression he had when he saw Mr Grace through the lens of his adult and experienced eyes. He is immersed so much in the experience that he substitutes his young past identity for his present adult one. However, his acts of remembering are a combination of the two times and selves. Thus, he narrates what he remembers from the past together with what he understands from his remembering. In other words, his acts of remembering include the memories he had and the ones he fabricates based on the holes or voids in his exiting memories. For example, in his recounting of the first time he saw Mr Grace, Max Morden interprets his experience:

> As he turned back to the house his eye caught mine and he winked. He did not do it in the way that adults usually did, at once arch and ingratiating. No, this was a comradely, a conspiratorial wink, masonic, almost, as if this moment that we, two strangers, adult and boy, had shared, although outwardly without significance, without content, even, nevertheless had meaning. (Banville 6)

Max Morden makes his memories meaningful through storying them. Additionally, his storytelling helps him solve some cognitive and emotion dilemmas with which he has been living a long time since he first experienced them.

Morden's memories of his wife's death as a result of cancer is one of the events of which the mental and emotional impact has not left him. Storying such a "dissembling" memory helps him to overcome the impact of anxiety which has been outliving the experience. He remembers the first time his wife's doctor told them of her disease:

> It was as if a secret had been imparted to us so dirty, so nasty, that we could hardly bear to remain in one another's company yet were unable to break free, each knowing the foul thing that the other knew and bound together by that very knowledge. From this day forward all would be dissembling. There would be no other way to live with death. (Banville 22)

In recounting the memories related to his matrimonial life and its termination by his wife's death, Max Morden highlights the power of intermentality between themselves. In other words, he highlights the function of, to use Alan Palmer's terminology, intersubjective first mind or intermental thought in which "thinking is joint, group, shared, or collective, as opposed to intramental, or individual or private thought (41). However, his storying of the experience enables him to "break free" of the "dirty" "secret" and "live with" the unbearable burden of his companion's "death" through retelling his tragic experience (Banville 22).

Despite the ultimate sense of certainty in his discourse of the past, Max Morden is anxious about the transient and fading nature of his memory as a result of a noticeable decline in his remembering ability as revealed in his discourse: "I am losing track of the millennia" (Banville 5). His acts of remembering, therefore, include the remembered and the forgotten pieces of his past life. In other words, despite the few traces left from his past life, it is the mental retaining of his experiences that forces Max to talk:

> The Cedars has retained hardly anything of the past, of the part of the past that I knew here. I had hoped for something definite of the Graces, no matter how small or seemingly insignificant, a faded photo, say, forgotten in a drawer, a lock of hair, or even a hair-pin, lodged between the floorboards, but there was nothing, nothing like that. No remembered atmosphere, either, to speak of. I suppose so many of the living passing through — it is a lodging house, after all — have worn away all traces of the dead. (Banville 39)

Storytelling, therefore, is presented as an act of repair for the narrator in *The Sea*. He fictionalizes his past life so that he might be satisfied with the plausible outcomes of his subjective effort. He rolls over his conjectures about the possible implications of his memories from which he cannot get away as they evoke a "pricking sensation" (Banville 41) in him. In doing so, he unavoidably reviews, as well as evaluates, his younger self's behaviour: "Odd, how often I see myself like this these days, at a distance, being someone else and doing things that only someone else would do" (Banville 43).

As mentioned, the presence of the Graces in Max Morden's life shaped the manner of his mental functioning both in the past and present. In his early adolescent years, his mind functioned based on fantasizing. It provided him with an alternative escape world. This quality has been developing in him since his childhood as a result of his living conditions. Dreaming about Mrs. Grace, for example, helped him escape the violent home environment:

> my mother and father in the front room fighting, as they did when they thought I was asleep, going at each other in a grinding undertone, every night, every night, until at last one night my father left us, never to return. But that was in winter, and somewhere else, and years off still. To keep from trying to hear what they were saying I distracted myself by making up dramas in which I rescued Mrs. Grace from some great and general catastrophe, a shipwreck or a devastating storm, and sequestered her for safety in a cave, conveniently dry and warm, where in moonlight — the liner had gone down by now, the storm had abated — I tenderly helped her out of her sopping swimsuit and wrapped a towel around her phosphorescent nudity, and we lay down and she leaned her head on my arm and touched my face in gratitude and sighed, and so we went to sleep together, she and I, lapped about by the vast soft summer night. (Banville 72-73)

Through Mrs. Grace, Max's mind acquires the art of inhabiting simultaneously two opposing realms of the real and unreal:

> She was wholly real, thick-meated, edible, almost. This was the most remarkable thing of all, that she was at once a wraith of my imagination and a woman of unavoidable flesh and blood, of fibre and musk and milk. My hitherto hardly less than seemly dreams of rescue and amorous dalliance had by now become riotous fantasies, vivid and at the same time hopelessly lacking in essential detail, of being voluptuously overborne by her, of sinking to the ground under all her warm weight, of being rolled, of being ridden, between her thighs, my arms pinned against my breast and my face on fire, at once her demon lover and her child. (Banville 88)

He finds many "odd things" in his imagining of his younger self's attraction to Mrs. Grace. He finds it "odd" that his "passion for Mrs.

Grace [...] fizzled out almost in the same moment that it achieved what might be considered its apotheosis" (Banville 108). He thus presents Mrs. Grace as on object of his adolescent desire which was both present and absent, or reality and fiction.

Max Morden's acts of remembering, accordingly, focus on the impact of his memories more than on the memories themselves. For example, although he has forgotten the physical features of his first sweetheart, who plays the central role in his storytelling, he tries to recount his experience with her through some vague patches of memory:

> Her [Chloe Grace's] hands. Her eyes. Her bitten fingernails. All this I remember, intensely remember, yet it is all disparate, I cannot assemble it into a unity. Try as I may . . . I am unable to conjure her as I can her mother, say, or Myles . . . I cannot, in short, see her. She wavers before my memory's eye at a fixed distance, always just beyond focus, moving backward at exactly the same rate as I am moving forward. (Banville 104)

*The Sea* begins with the narrator's presence in the Cedars and ends with his leaving there. Along with his physical journey, the narrator also experiences a mental journey in which he examines his experiences as well his identity. Unlike his desperate mood at the beginning where he presents himself as a blocked author who "has got no farther than half of a putative first chapter [a big book on Bonnard] and a notebook filled with derivative and half-baked would-be aperçus," as a result of his remembering process and examination of the nature of subjective phenomena such as memory and knowing, he sees some new "possibilities" (Banville 259 and 260) on the horizon. When a nurse informs the narrator of his wife's death at the end of *The Sea*, he feels as if "walking into the sea" (Banville 264). Throughout his acts of remembering, Max Morden's mind functions in a similar way to the sea—pulsating. However, his examination of some episodes from his past life through remembering them brings about a personal reconciliation. By the end of his storytelling, which can only present a shadow of the past, he learns to embrace or accept his life in the past and move forward. Such a narrative quality, as it is shown in the next chapter, is also the main outcome of the narrator's storytelling activity in Anne Enright's *The Gathering*.

# THREE
# Fictions of the Past:
# Memory and Imagination in Anne Enright's *The Gathering*

> "[O]ur past follows us, becoming larger and larger with the present it picks up on its way; and consciousness means memory."
> (Henri Bergson 137)

Anne Enright (1962- ), in Heidi Hansson's words, "has been hailed as one of the most exciting contemporary Irish writers, praised for her lyrical, evocative language and her original style" (216). However, as Hansson observes, Enright has a unique place in Irish literature since she does not fit into the studies of contemporary Irish literature because of, on the one hand, her ostensible avoidance of the "issues of national identity and the state of Irish society that informs so much of current criticism" and, on the other hand, her "fragmented storytelling" (216). Thus, Hansson calls Enright a "postnationalist" writer by arguing that "Enright's narrative strategies as well as the themes she tackles can be linked to a position beyond nationalism. [...] postnationalism is defined by dissonance and divergence in contradistinction to the uniformity of nationalist thought" (219). Likewise, "From the start," as Liam Harte holds, "Enright's fiction announced itself as both postmodernist and feminist" (*Reading* 218)[5]. The two qualities which resonate dissonance and divergence are also the defining qualities of the central character's acts of remembering in Enright's *The Gathering*, which is, according to Carol Dell'Amico, her "testimonial" (59).

---

[5] Like Hansson and Harte, Bridget English also highlights the high frequency of postmodernist approaches to the novel: "Many critics would classify *The Gathering*'s style as postmodernist owing to the novel's fragmented structure that deliberately resists assimilation into linear narrative, along with the self-conscious mode of narration, dark humor, and suspicion of the authority of grand narratives" (151).

As a witness to the molestation scene of her brother in childhood, the narrator in *The Gathering* struggles to remember the details of her memory of the event. Her episodic memory, however, lacks certainty and is heavily based on speculations. She makes up stories, or fake memories, so that she might construct a meaningful narrative of what happened in the past. Most of her memories are fictional, constructed, or inauthentic.

Narration of trauma plays the central role in the critical approaches to *The Gathering*. "[S]tudies of ... *The Gathering*," says Costello-Sullivan, "often focus on the text's narrative representation of trauma and traumatic memory" (*Trauma* 54). According to Ellen McWilliams, *The Gathering* is a "working through of individual and family traumas" (189). The narrative is mostly understood as a medium through which the writer-narrator attempts to overcome traumatic memories. In *The Gathering*, says Bridget English, "[i]t is this gap between the past and the present that most interests Enright, as it mirrors the holes in memory created by traumatic experience that must be repeated in order to be overcome" (150). As expressed in "Enright's experimental style and structure," the narrator's trauma, in English's words, ends in "the ruptures in [her] memory" (179). However, the reliability and retrievability of memory together with the narrator's perspective towards it, and the defining role of the narrator's acts of remembering in her sense of identity have not received due attention and/or appreciation in critical approaches to Enright's work.

Memory is the main subject in *The Gathering*, a narrative recounted in the mode of autobiographical memory. Enright in this novel, as argued by English, "uses postmodern techniques such as the self-conscious and unreliable narrator to call into question the nature of memory" (152). In other words, one of Veronica Hegarty's important problems is the "unreliability of memory" (English 165). The narrative plot in Enright's novel revolves around the consequences of a traumatic past experience—paedophilia or child abuse. The novel, in Jean-Michel Ganteau's words, "clearly digs into the depths of collective trauma and takes part in the general process of unearthing the hidden, and of voicing what was silenced for many years" (182). Veronica's storytelling is a form of reaction to a changed sociocultural situation which acts as a trigger in her narrative construction of the Liam-related stories:

> Over the next twenty years, the world around us changed and I remembered Mr Nugent. But I never would have made that shift on my own—if I hadn't been listening to the radio, and reading the paper, and hearing about what went on in schools and churches and in people's homes. It went on slap-bang in front of me and still I did not realise it. And for this, I am very sorry too. (Enright 172-173)

However, although Ganteau, following several other commentators, analyses *The Gathering* as "some state-of-the-nation novel" (183), as it is argued in this chapter, it is the personal consequences of a traumatic childhood event which mostly drives the narrative. The represented acts of remembering in *The Gathering* all turn upon a traumatic childhood experience, or a "wound of family" (Enright 243), by narrating which the first-person writer-narrator hopes to achieve a gradual recovery. "In the case of Enright and many other contemporary Irish novelists," as Kathleen Costello-Sullivan observes, "the possibility for recovery lies in acknowledging the materiality and experiential dimensions of family relationships, particularly mother-child relationships, and in allowing the imperfections of lived, physical familial experience to replace the 'spectral femininity' of idealized and erased motherhood that has often been Irish fiction's key symbol for the domestic reverberations of trauma" ("Trauma" 404). Thus, according to Costello-Sullivan, *The Gathering* "effects a kind of gendered intervention into the experience of trauma" (*Trauma* 54). However, as this study argues and as is also true of the two other narratives analysed in the present book, the narrator's remembering game can be analysed as the main narrative focus in *The Gathering*.

Although most of the represented memories in *The Gathering* are elusive or only partially retrievable because of either their absence or the unwillingness of the narrator as the remembering agent, "the novel," as Ganteau highlights in his conclusion, "thanks to the welter of remembrance acts and events, presents the narrator and the reader with a glimmer of hope, with the end of the novel hinting at the possibility of the end of both melancholia and mourning. Remembrance as act and event is thus instrumental in healing and working through" (198). By relying on her episodic memories, the thirty-nine-year-old Veronica Hegarty writes her autobiography so that she can make sense of her own identity and past life through the retrieved, recollected, and/or (re)constructed memories.

*The Gathering* is a narrative of the past. By covering more than seven decades (from 1925 (beginning of the story) to 1998 (time of narration). The past, as the narrator contends, "is not a happy place" (Enright 233). Veronica's story is, therefore, about the effects of some unhappy events in her past life. In other words, it is her biological history, "History is only biological—that's what I think. We pick and choose the facts about ourselves—where we came from and what it means" (Enright 162). One part of Veronica's character lies in the past, her "another part" (Enright 113) that constantly calls her attention to itself. The territory of the latter part is the present time and to some extent the future time which is unknown and unimaginable to her: "I feel the future falling through the roof of my mind and when I look nothing is there. A rope. Something dangling in a bag, that I cannot touch" (Enright 39). Thus, her mind is under the control of the past.

Veronica's storytelling and acts of remembering are her attempts to investigate the past. It is the historical and fictional biography of herself and some of her family members that make her mind busy. Thus, she is determined to write histories down in order to reveal secrets about herself and the others because for Veronica "history is such a romantic place, with its jarveys and urchins and side-buttoned boots." However, it is repeating itself eternally in her mind: "If it would just stay still, I think, and settle down. If it would just stop sliding around in my head" (Enright 13).

Made up of thirty-nine parts, *The Gathering* is about the narrator's troubled relationships with the past and with her family members (grandmother, mother, brother, and husband). More importantly, prompted by a dire childhood traumatic secret, it is about the suicidal death of the narrator's brother. The represented and constructed memories in *The Gathering* are triggered by the narrator's desire to discover a buried past. Her brother's death initiates Veronica's narration. She begins writing her narrative right after her favourite brother's death, and in doing so she tells us about the past, the present and the future without following a chronological order.

Having "used to be a journalist" (Enright 39), Veronica makes up her story through the narration as well as creation of memories. She narrates her memories of the iconic events in her past and whenever she fails to do so, she creates a related possible memory in order to fill the existing void. She is unsatisfied with her past life and her storytelling is the expression of her desire to change it: "If it would be possible to unbuild it all and start again" (Enright 24). Her memories are at the service of her narrative construction. In other words, her creation of memory is presented as a narrative technique which helps her to make up a united whole out of fragmented parts. She vividly remembers some events besides aligning her memories of them to her desired rearrangement of her past life so that she might be satisfied with the result. Her narration, therefore, is her intentional intervention against the uncontrollable nature of her mind and imagination. Her disorganized, disintegrated, and circular mode of narration represents her mental state too. To put it differently, Veronica remembers both to be aware of the events in the past and to overcome her present situation. She remembers so that she might go beyond her nightmares and find peace. She is haunted and surrounded by the dead souls. She is a neurotic and sleepwalker.

Veronica feels detached and depressed while telling her story. She calls herself, "A disruption of the natural order, that is what I am" (Enright 43). The source of her inner conflict is the conflict she has had with the outside world: "I am in a rage with every single one of my brothers and sisters, ... and I am boiling mad with Liam for being dead too, just now, when I need him most. Quite literally, I am beyond myself. I am so angry I have a second view of the kitchen" (Enright 10). Similarly, she experiences an emotional divorce from her husband: "The last time I touched him was the night of Liam's wake. And I don't know what is wrong with me since, but I do not believe in my husband's body any more" (Enright 73). What matters to her husband is irrelevant to her: "Tom [...] dreams of hurt and redemption in the world of corporate finance, and it is all nothing to do with me" (Enright 36). As within her own mind she oscillates between the past and the present, in her matrimonial life too she dangles between her desire to be a normal wife and not to be one at the same time: "What else can I do? We could not afford a divorce. Besides I do not want to leave him. I cannot sleep with him, that is all. So my husband is waiting for me to sleep with him again, and I am waiting for something else. I am waiting for things to become clear" (Enright 37).

Veronica has a disquieted and confused mind at the beginning of her storytelling. Triggered by her brother's suicide, her mind is caught up with what happened to him when they were children. She defines herself as a person with "the ordinary life of the brain" (Enright 175). However, she is exposed to some thoughts over which she does not have any control: "there are little thoughts in your head that can grow until they eat your entire mind. Just tiny little thoughts — they are like a cancer, there is no telling what triggers the spread, or who will be struck, and why some get it and others are spared. [...] we fill up sometimes, like those little wooden birds that sit on a pole — we fill up with it, until *donk*, we tilt into the drink" (Enright 175).

Veronica's narration in *The Gathering* is a long process of her subjective experiencing of some iconic events happened in the past. Presentation of a series of acts of remembering in Enright's narrative begins with the narrator's questioning regarding the authenticity of memory itself. Her critical perspective towards memory and the constructing role of her imagination in it are revealed from the opening sentences of the narrative:

> I would like to write down what happened in my grandmother's house the summer I was eight or nine, but I am not sure if it really did happen. I need to bear witness to an uncertain event. I feel it roaring inside me — this thing that may not have taken place. I don't even know what name to put on it. I think you might call it a crime of the flesh, but the flesh is long fallen away and I am not sure what hurt may linger in the bones. (Enright 1)

The fact that the narrator's acts of remembering do not have the potential to reveal the truth is a parallel narrative subject in *The Gathering* besides its main theme of recounting the real events and their destructive effects on the narrator and her recently died brother Liam. Thus, she is recollecting and creating a memorial narrative of the past too.

Veronica's memories are full of contradictions, refutations, and voids. She has a critical view of her own memories. She narrates her memories and, at the same time, disqualifies them. On the one hand, she should recount her memories as they connect her to her past life and in this way help her to conceptualize a personal identity for herself. On the other hand, she knows her available memories do not present the truth. For example, her account of the time in her childhood when with her two siblings she stayed at Ada's includes both her recollection and realizations:

> I couldn't tell you what Nugent did, though it has stuck somewhere in my head that he was a bookie, or a bookie's clerk, that he put on a grey cashmere coat from time to time, and got into a black car, and was driven to the racecourse. All I really know is that he used the garage out the back for his old jalopies and you never knew if he was in there or not. I thought — if I thought anything at the time — that Ada allowed him to use it because she had no car of her own, and by that time, Charlie did not drive. (Enright 104)

Veronica, thus, is a self-conscious storyteller. Suffering from sleeplessness and depression, her writing is a conscious attempt to overcome her own mental problems. She cannot go beyond some of her childhood memories. She is used to "imagining things, or even remembering them" (Enright 90), and is aware of the irretrievability of the experienced events as well as the abstractness of the truth: "I do not know the truth, or I do not know how to tell the truth. All I have are stories, night thoughts, the sudden convictions that uncertainty spawns. All I have are ravings, […] I stay downstairs while the family breathes above me and I write it down, I lay them out in nice sentences, all my clean, white bones" (Enright 2). However, she does not have a choice other than telling, and pretending to tell, what happened and/or what might have happened. In this sense,

"As a ghost story," in Fintan O'Toole's words, *The Gathering* represents "the sense of being haunted [...and] the sense of being displaced" (107).

Despite her intention to find out the truth through her storytelling and acts of remembering, Veronica's narrative of the past has some elements of metafiction as she is aware of the fading of her memories through time. Lack of certainty is the main feature of her storying the past: "Maybe I am wrong" (Enright 47). Thus, her narration is an intentional act of rearranging the sequence of events in her past life. For example, in remembering a memory from her childhood, she immediately discredits her own account:

> [A] priest marked Kitty's upper arm with a ring of bruises, giving us, as he held on to her, a lecture on wickedness that was dense with rage. And I cannot remember a single word of it, or what Ada later said about the state of Kitty's arm, though I do recall the thick, vivid quality of the priest's mouthing face, like undiluted fruit squash. And though common sense says that these two events should not have happened on the same day, I say that they did. (Enright 50)

Since her memory system has some holes and is full of gaps, it is her storytelling rather than telling the truth based on the facts in her memories that control her mind. In her own words, she "remember[s] in the gap" (Enright 72), and "there is something immoral about the mind's eye" (Enright 91).

Veronica's prime aim of storytelling, as she admits it at the end of her narrative, is to restore the normal order to her private and social lives: "I do not want a different life. I just want to be able to live it, that's all. I want to wake up in the morning and fall asleep at night. I want to make love to my husband again" (Enright 260). Her recollection and construction of memories are supposed to clear up the state of confusion in her mind by establishing in her "Some new soul" (Enright 260) although the final sentence in her narrative does not imply that. Having been sitting in Gatwick airport in London waiting to return home, she feels the imminent threat: "I have been falling for months. I have been falling into my own life, for months. And I am about to hit it now" (Enright 261).

Discovering the truth is the most important return of Veronica's narrative. By the end of her narrative, she feels willing to reveal, although partially, the truth about Liam as a result of her long imagining process and acts of remembering. She uses storytelling as a medium to find the truth and, as a result of her ultimate belief in the obtained truth, is willing to share it with her family:

> I know what I have to do — even though it is too late for the truth, I will tell the truth. I will get hold of Ernest and tell him what happened to Liam in Broadstone, and I will ask him to break this very old news to the rest of the family (but don't tell Mammy!) because I cannot do it myself, I do not have the arguments for it. I just couldn't face Bea's disapproval, or Ita's dank sorrow, or Ivor, crisply saying, 'How come you guys had all the fun?' God, I hate my family, these people I never chose to love, but love all the same. (Enright 259)

The suicidal death of Veronica's favourite brother triggers her narration and evaluation of some family-related issues. However, more than recounting her memories by relying on the facts, she constructs a story based on her creative imagination because the evidence or facts are either missing in what she can remember, or they are beyond her age and experience. Thus, her active mind is full of real and unreal family memories. The self-proclaimed obligation to find the truth on the one hand and the impossibility of doing so through her memories on the other occupy the foundation of her mental state while recounting her autobiographical story. The past events linger in her memories without giving place to new experiences. In other words, her past life does not let her go: "I look at the hills, trying to grow up, trying to let my father die, trying to let my sister enter her adolescence (never mind menopause). And none of these things is possible. None of them. There is a line on the landscape that refuses to move, it slides backwards instead, and that is where I fix my eye" (Enright 43-44). However, as discussed in the two following parts, by the end of her remembering process Veronica achieves the goals based on which her storytelling stands. If not based on real or historical evidence, she finds out the truth regarding Nugent's sexual abuse of her brother Liam by the help of her creative imagination and constructed memory. Her act of storytelling also helps her to establish experiencing a new, more positive, mental state through facilitating her return to normal life.

## 3.1 Remembering as an Act of Memory Formation

Storytelling in *The Gathering* is a long act of remembering. In a similar way to a detective, the narrator primarily searches for documentary evidence about the manner of a possible event in the past through her acts of remembering. In failing to do so, she uses her inventive and imaginative mind to create a pseudo-real version of the event through the unreal or fake memories. Before her storytelling activity, as she acknowledges, she did not "hold or remember the thing she saw." Thus, she thought she "had forgotten it entirely" (Enright 172). Her remembering, therefore, is generally an aspirational act in narrative which mostly happens based on possibilities rather than certainties. In other words, on the one hand her act of remembering is the main device used in her battle against forgetting, and on the other hand it is the background against which she produces fictional versions of some events. Her memories are mixed with her imagination. Her accounts of Ada and Liam are the stories equally made up of fact and fiction. Since she cannot capture the truth at the core of her recounting, she represents the possibilities. Therefore, she fills in voids both in her memories and in her narrative too.

Veronica has a weak memory even though she retells a few of her memories in "vivid technicolour" (Enright 166). However, since there are "sudden slack[s]" in her "mental map" (Enright 158), she does not remember so many details in her stories: "I don't remember the hospital" (Enright 115); "What did we talk about? I wish I knew" (Enright 118); "I wish I could remember what exactly he said, but conversation doesn't stick to my memory of Liam" (Enright 118); "It was the summer, and sometimes we were still talking when the sun came up—but I have no idea what these conversations were" (Enright 118); "I remember it as you might remember a scene from a film" (Enright 120). Thus, she tries to remember the details regarding the defining moments/events in her past life: "I wish I could remember what made me sit up and throw my things in the case, and leave: I fancy a piece of distant birdsong; the sense of someone calling me home, but the only person who might call was Liam and he was nowhere to be seen" (Enright 121).

Veronica makes up a fictional past in her pseudo-report of the past. She creates a story by arranging the events in her desired order. Then, she disrupts the constructed order by rearranging her already completed narrative construction of the past. In other words, she pretends to be remembering on the one hand, and to be disremembering on the other one. By doing so, she keeps us alert through her storytelling activity. Therefore, within the fictional world of *The Gathering*, fiction itself among the main themes. The narrator fictionalizes the past under the pretext of her memories. Her act of remembering is in fact her narrative technique which allows her to tell us her story. For example, her grandmother-related memories are mostly fake and fiction-like narratives. Veronica tries to understand Ada's life, and why she did what she did: "I do not know why Ada married Charlie when it was Nugent who had her measure. And though you could say that she did not marry Nugent because she did not like him, that is not really enough. We do not always like the people we love—we do not always have that choice" (Enright 110). Her story of Ada's life and marriage is based on some of her cognitive biases, what she refers to as "imputations"—"Ada has suffered enough from our imputations" (Enright 207). She first fabricates a background for her grandmother. Then, she makes her judgement about her own story by her mindreading effort in the absence of the analysand: "Maybe that was her mistake. She thought she could choose. She thought she could marry someone she liked and be happy with him, and have happy children. She did not realise that every choice is fatal. For a woman like Ada, every choice is an error, as soon as it is made" (Enright 110).

The apex of Veronica's memory construction is the imagined biography she creates for her grandmother Ada by imagining a past beyond her own life through sharing with us her own "picture of 'the orphan Ada Merriman'" (Enright 90). Constructed memory softens her hatred against Ada by providing a chance to examine her behaviour and life from a different perspective. In other words, she begins sympathising with her grandmother by saying, "Life was hard for my grandmother, I know that now" (Enright 89). She tells us about the time she began "imagining" things about her grandmother:

> [I]t was at Ada's sink, in Broadstone [...] Standing at that Belfast sink, with the view of the yard and the green door to the garage beyond, I imagined Ada with her suitcase at nine years old, or ten, or whatever age she was when her mother died and she faced the wide world alone. I tried to imagine a father for her, but I could not. I imagined my own mother dying at home in Griffith Way—over and over again, actually—Mammy died, and my father wept and died, and afterwards, when she was planted, I imagined great adventures for myself and Liam, now that we were orphans too. (Enright 90)

As she does in her narrative, she has been using the technique of imagining to fill in the blanks.

Constructing memory is as important as recounting memory in Veronica's embedded narrative of Ada-Lamb-Liam. In her desire to reveal the truth, Veronica constructs a biography for her grandmother based on what she knows about her properties. Thus, the main part of Ada Merriman-Lambert Nugent's embedded narrative is a fabrication based on Veronica's imaginings. The outcome is essential for her narrative of Liam. The overall plot in the Ada-related narrative is constructed based on who Ada and Lamb were, what they did as well as the effects of their behaviour on the Hogartys' lives.

Ada's and Nugent's shared and personal stories play a fundamental role in Veronica's acts of remembering. Most of her memories happen in Ada's home in the garage of which she thinks Nugent sexually assaulted her then nine-year-old brother Liam in 1968, the year her grandfather died too. Before presenting her real and unreal memories of Nugent's abuse, Veronica fabricates a related history. She presents us her episodic memory of Ada, Nugent, and her grandfather Charlie Spillane: "The seeds of my brother's death were sown many years ago. The person who planted them is long dead—at least that's what I think. So if I want to tell Liam's story, then I have to start long before he was born. And, in fact, this is the tale that I would love to write" (Enright 13). Thus, she mostly "write[s] about Ada and Nugent in the Belvedere, endlessly, over and again" (Enright 38).

In storying their relationship, Veronica constructs a background for Ada's and Lamb's lifelong affinity. Not knowing the history of her grandmother's marriage, she fabricates a story. Veronica delivers an imaginary account of the moment when in 1925 for the first time the nineteen-year-old Ada sees Lamb Nugent and her future husband Charlie Spillane in the Belvedere Hotel. She highlights Ada's reservedness and deceiving coyness which helped her control the two men's behaviour in such a way that finally her "stillness becomes triumphant" (Enright 17). As is true about her overall acts of remembering, Veronica's Ada-related-narrative, however, is dubious in nature. For example, she cannot say with certainty what happened in her grandmother's first meeting with Lamb Nugent, "Or maybe she won't [look at Lamb Nugent]. Nothing has been said. No one has moved. It is possible that Nugent is imagining it all — or that I am. Maybe he is a pathetic thing at twenty-three; all hand-wrung tweed cap and Adam's apple; maybe Ada doesn't even notice him there across the room" (Enright 17). Similarly, despite her arbitrary ascriptions of goals and intentions to Ada, she cannot say why Ada did what she did when she met Lamb for the first time. In this case, her reasoning is a heap of egoistic possibilities: "But this is 1925. A man. A woman. She must know what lies ahead of them now. She knows because she is beautiful. She knows because of all the things that have happened since. She knows because she is my Granny" (Enright 17). She reveals Ada's mysterious and unpredictable character by stating that unlike what the appearances were, she "married" Lamb's friend Charlie Spillane, and by adding "not just because he had a car," (Enright 229) Veronica implies the materialistic and opportunistic nature of her grandmother. However, despite what happened, Lamb Nugent was so stubborn that he never left Ada throughout his life: "But he never left her. My grandmother was Lamb Nugent's most imaginative act. I may not forgive him, but it is this — the way he stayed true to it — that defines the man most, for me" (Enright 22). In her comment on the nature of Ada's relationship with the two men after her marriage, Veronica implies her immorality: "So Nugent is the lover in all this,

Charlie is the transport, Ada is the wraith and lilith the lovely girl the fallen woman the sad whore the poor orphan the safe bet, whatever way you look at it" (Enright 106).

In furthering their constant and clandestine relationship, Veronica imagines Ada and Lamb "young again" (Enright 138) — when Ada is forty-seven and Lamb fifty-one — and constructs the possible romance between them by ascribing to them feeling, thoughts, and intentions. In doing so, she initiates a mindreading process as she tries to reveal their thoughts and feelings about the constantly repressed desire between themselves. She "only suppose[s]" (Enright 17) a possible "romance" (Enright 21) between them, and narrates whatever she likes to happen in their relationship:

> Ada knows that he is sad, but she has yet to sympathise. Lamb Nugent has a wife, Kathleen, and four healthy children. He has no cause for complaint. What he asks is what Ada refuses most to give, he asks her to believe in his grief, the ordinary grief of a man with a wife he does not love overmuch and four children who he does not, for a moment, understand; the usual grief of men when they find that they have done nothing, and there is nothing left for them to do. He wants her to pity him his perfectly pleasant life, and the fact that it does not belong to him; the fact that he is a ghost in his own house, looking at his wife, who drives him up the wall, and his four children, who rob each breath as it comes out of his mouth. While he sits here with a woman too old to bed, the keeper of his treasures, the woman who will not love him, though she really knows she should. (Enright 135-136)

Thus, in her imaginary narrative of Ada and Nugent, Veronica "allow[s] them" (Enright 138) to do whatever she thinks they had desired to do but could not and/or did not do because of their situation and, more importantly, because of Ada's self-centred and unsympathetic character. Thus, she constructs their relationship based on the presupposition that the apparent love between them is more like jeering than the authentic kind: "The air between them is too thin for love," because "The only thing that can be thrown across the air of Dublin town is a kind of jeering" (Enright 16).

Storying the past brings Veronica to the conclusion she had it ready complete in her mind from the very beginning. Her story is not intended to share with us the dark aspects of Ada's past life. Rather, it is designed to reveal the evil nature of her character —

how lack of empathy and love in her character brought about the whole tragedy in the storyworld, and how Ada is the only responsible person for Liam's suicidal death as her sense of love is "wanting":

> They know too, that this moment is long past — they are not young, and there is nothing fateful about a coupling, when it is too late. What lies ahead is not so much a fork in the road as a small lay-by. They might do this, and it would not matter. Nothing would be changed by it; neither the future nor the past. Nugent would still have loved Ada, or wanted her, and Ada would still want Charlie, whether she loved him or not — whether, indeed, she ever loved anybody, or not. This is a difficult question for her to answer at forty-seven, and it is the one that is raised by Nugent's hand to her hip: the question of whether she ever loved anybody, her vagrant husband, or her children, or herself, or the parents she never had.
> What of it? Ada does not love people so much as feed them and keep them clean, and this is a form of loving too, but he has sucked it out of her, this man with his four healthy children and his perfectly nice wife, he has taken her domestic love and found it wanting, and for a moment Ada does not recognise the lie — that all women are heartless because they are desired. For a moment, Ada stands there and thinks that it is true (and perhaps it is true), she has never loved a single soul. She is alone. There is nothing left for her to do. (Enright 138-139)

Veronica is aware of the border between reality and fiction in her story. However, based on some available signs, she fabricates an alternative reality which serves her desire: "Still, I would like to allow them more. Ada has three children, Nugent four, and though it is possible to endure these bodily events as though they were happening to someone else (as my own mother might have done) I don't think it was in Ada's character, or in his, to be so innocent" (Enright 138). The represented reality is an effect of the fictional side of her story constructed mainly by her mind's eye. As she highlights, "There is no shift between my mind's eye and my real eye" (Enright 158).

Veronica herself is aware of the constructed nature of Ada's and Lamb's narrative. However, by using the metaphors of "whore" and "bookie" and through following them into their most private space, she tries to reveal the banality of their deeds and characters:

> I would like to think something else happened, when he entered her. But I do not know what. They were in love, suddenly. Or they were in pain. Or what? [...]
> The bookie fucks the whore (I had forgotten she was a whore), and we are near to the truth of it here, we are getting to the *truth* of it — of man's essential bookieness and woman's essential whoreishness — we are pushing for it now as Nugent pushes into Ada, the fact of her baseness, the fact that *she wants it too*. Or is this enough? Would he not, to prove his point, need to do more?
> I can twist them as far as you like, here on the page; make them endure all kinds of protraction, bliss, mindlessness, abjection, release. I can bend and reconfigure them in the rudest possible ways, but my heart fails me, there is something so banal about things that happen *behind closed doors*, these terrible transgressions that are just sex after all. (emphasis original, Enright 139-140)

Veronica blames Ada for the Hegarty's shame: "This is the moment for blame [...] we realise that it was Ada's fault all along" (Enright 223). In her mind, Ada is "always at cross purposes to the world" (Enright 98). As in the past or in the time of story, Ada seems to her both "loving" and "horrible" (Enright 17) at the time of narration. Although mainly established based on the vague and absent evidence, her negative perspective controls her narrative of Ada at the beginning: "When I was in college, I decided that Ada had been a prostitute — the way you do. It must have been around the time she died" (Enright 84).

Veronica's heartless evaluation of Ada's character also transforms her acts of remembering as well as the construction of unreal memories. She tries to sympathise with the young grandmother who had left her family and had to survive alone: "How she [Ada] turned and carried the suitcase out of the house. And everything that seemed impossible was possible after all. She had the gift of feet, that placed themselves one after the other so that she could walk out of there, and she had the gift of her hands, to make her way through life, and she did not look back" (Enright 253). Despite her efforts, Veronica fails to retrieve the real Ada through recounting and constructing of memories as she finds out that Ada belongs to the past just like a ghost: "Ada first, pragmatically dead. A thin old thing, she is the kind of ghost who is always turning away. Ada just gets on with being dead. The past is a puddle around her feet"

(Enright 215). However, Ada continues to haunt her just like a real person: "I see her not as I 'saw' the ghosts on the stairs. I see her as I might see an actual woman standing in the light of the hall" (Enright 217). In other words, Veronica remains under Ada's gaze: "Ada's eyes are crawling down my shoulder and my back. Her gaze is livid down one side of me; it is like a light: my skin hardens under it and crinkles like a burn" (Enright 221).

Despite creating different possible scenarios, Veronica fails to read Ada's mind about what happened to Lamb: "When I try to remember, or imagine that I remember, looking into Ada's face with Lamb Nugent's come spreading over my hand, I can only conjure a blank, or her face as a blank. At most, there is a word written on Ada's face, and that word is, 'Nothing'" (Enright 222). Thus, her remembering leads her to accept the fact that the past is gone, and the truth of what happened in the past will always be vague and fictional. In a scene at the end of narrative, Veronica is standing at the sea and based on her memories is dreaming of buying Ada's house, renovating it, and selling it. At the basis of seeing such a "film" (Enright 239) lies her desire to get rid of her memories about what might have happened at Ada's house. Thus, she no longer blames her for what happened to her brother: "I do not blame her. And I don't know why that is" (Enright 223).

In a similar way to her narrative of Ada, Veronica's narration of Lambert Nugent is a total fabrication or reassembling: "He [Lambert Nugent] must be reassembled; click clack; his muscles hooked to bone and wrapped with fat, the whole skinned over and dressed in a suit of navy or brown—something about the cut of the lapels, maybe, that is a little too sharp, and the smell on his hands would be already a little finer than carbolic" (Enright 14). After a long deviation from the main topic of her narrative, she returns to her main topic by saying, "It is time to put an end to the shifting stories and the waking dreams. It is time to call an end to romance and just say what happened in Ada's house, the year that I was eight and Liam was barely nine" (Enright 142). In a similar way to her act of remembering of Ada-Nugent, Veronica's memory of Liam-Nugent is made up of fragmented, fabricated patches through which she tries to find out how at her grandmother's house, which belonged to

Nugent, Nugent molested and possibly raped her brother. All in all, she remembers Lamb Nugent as "evil" (Enright 222) and is sure that "Nugent was horrible to my brother in ordinary ways, too, out there. He had his sadisms, I am sure, and his methods" (Enright 223).

Lamb Nugent's horrible image never disappears from her mind although her conclusions about what he might have done to her brother are only her speculations intended to shed light on the darkness of both his character and his action:

And on the other side of me is the welcoming darkness of Lambert Nugent. I am facing into that darkness and falling. I am holding his old penis in my hand.

> But it is a very strange picture. It is made up of the words that say it. I think of the 'eye' of his penis, and it is pressing against my own eye. I 'pull' him and he keels towards me. I 'suck' him and from his mouth there protrudes a narrow, lemon sweet.
> This comes from a place in my head where words and actions are mangled. It comes from the very beginning of things, and I cannot tell if it is true. Or I cannot tell if it is real. But I am sickened by the evil of him all the same, I am sweltering in it. (Enright 221- 222)

Veronica the rememberer's mind is paralyzed with the ugliness of what Lamb did to her brother, "I cannot move. In this memory or dream, I can neither stop it, nor make it continue" (Enright 222). Therefore, unlike her conclusions about Ada, Veronica's remembering and reconstruction process in the Liam-Lamb narrative does not lead her to come to terms with what happened between the two. Like a wave, not only the horrible nature of his action repeats itself in her mind, but also it is spread to the outside world. In other words, his evil is universal. By the end of her narrative, Veronica blames Lamb as much as she blames the time in which his evil action happened: "I know he could be the explanation for all of our lives, and I know something more frightening still — that we did not have to be damaged by him in order to be damaged. It was the air he breathed that did for us. It was the way we were obliged to breathe his second-hand air" (Enright 224). Thus, as much as she assigns Lamb the responsibility of Liam's destruction, Veronica attributes it to the time they shared with Liam, when "Children were being chucked out all over Dublin" and "parents were mad" (Enright 96).

## 3.2 Veronica Hegarty's Forging of Identity through Memory Patches

Veronica Hegarty experiences a question of identity after her brother's sudden and unexpected death. She marks his death as the beginning point of her unsettlement: "I am in the horrors. It started sometime after the funeral" (Enright 133). The way she feels at the memorial gathering of her brother at the Church symbolically shows her feeling and thoughts about the distorted nature of her being: "Everyone wants a bit of me. And it has nothing to do with what I might want, or what my body might want, whatever that might be—God knows it is a long time since I knew. There I am, sitting on a church bench in my own meat: pawed, used, loved, and very lonely" (Enright 244). Veronica desires to be herself but cannot. Her identity is interwoven with that of her family. "[B]eing part of a family," for Veronica, "is the most excruciating possible way to be alive" (Enright 243). Thus, the same distorted I, which drives the narrative progression in *The Sea* and *Milkman*, has also a significant role in *The Gathering*, where at the centre of Veronica's acts of remembering lie her two selves—the older self (at the story time) and the historically constructed one (at the time of narration).

Liam's death renovates Veronica's past. "Death," as Bridget English argues, "calls into question the nature of memory" (152) in *The Gathering*. She defines herself as a person "who has lost something that cannot be replaced" (Enright 11) and as a person who does not "know what is wrong with being me" (Enright 184). In all her walking-at-night moments and acts of remembering, she wants to regain the "sanity and emptiness" of her mind (Enright 218) as it is replete with conflicting thoughts and memories. Therefore, her story is the story of her "mortified" (Enright 97) soul. She has had some unresolved (family) conflicts about which she is writing in her narrative—the conflicts with her parents, her siblings, Ada, Michael Weise, and above all the conflicting thoughts in her mind.

The narrator is in a constant battle within her own mind. Before telling her story, she has lost her entire belief in people and in memories too. However, her writing is increasingly oriented towards bringing her beliefs back: "I try to believe in something, […] I bow my head and try to believe that love will make it better, or if love won't then children will. I turn from the high to the humble and believe, for many seconds at a time, in the smallness and the necessity of being a mother" (Enright 228). Similarly, she tries to push back her negative thoughts about her husband. There is a big "gap" (Enright 177) between she and her husband: "I do not believe in Tom beside me: that he is alive (sometimes I wake to find him dead, only to wake again). Or that he loves me. Or that any of our memories are mutual. So he lies there, separate, while I lose faith" (Enright 133). She tries to regain her faith in people and life through re-examining her memories which provide her with a Cartesian chance to deconstruct and then construct her belief in herself and in the others too. For example, she tries to "save" (Enright 177) her marriage. Her two children also "did it [saving] for us, at least for a while" (Enright 180). However, all in all they had a troubled marital relationship as "it never really did get fixed" (Enright 181).

Her storytelling is her effort to overcome her mental problems, or "nightmares" (Enright 215), and to find out the meaning of her life besides her role in the lives of the others. In remembering a day when a nun named Sister Benedict told her the story of St. Veronica who "wiped the face of Christ on the road to Calvary and He left His face on her tea towel. Or the picture of His face" (Enright 128), she remembers how at that time she came to a different conclusion about herself: "I am not Veronica. Though I have done my fair share of wiping, in my day, and it is true that I am attracted to people who suffer, or men who suffer, my suffering husband, my suffering brother, the suffering figure of Mr Nugent. It is unfortunately true that happiness, in a man, does not do it, for me" (Enright 129).

The narrator's sense of identity becomes shattered after her brother's suicide. Functioning as an awakening event in the narrative, Liam's death triggers some ontological questions in the narrator. Hence, she writes/narrates her autobiography to understand her family and personal life. Her narration is a sign of her responsibility too. By reviewing some events in her childhood period, or in the story time, and in the adult one, or in the time of narration, she tries to find out where she missed what she should have done. Therefore, the narrator tries to define her own identity through her acts of remembering.

Veronica's acts of remembering include some embedded narratives which run coincidently, although at different times, throughout the narrative. One of them is her memories of her mother and her judgments about them. She criticizes her mother and tries to remember whatever she can about her. Her mother "escapes" her and is "fading" as well as a representation of "forgetfulness itself" (Enright 3). She describes her mother an invisible and "a vague person" who "can't even see herself" (Enright 4) and "guards whatever she has left of herself deep inside" (Enright 197). Similarly, Veronica does not "forgive" her mother (Enright 7-8) for what she claims as ignoring her motherly care and responsibilities. Through her criticism, Veronica blames her mother for her shortcomings, or for how she was not engaged in family issues since *"Don't tell Mammy.* It was the mantra of our childhoods, or one of them. *Don't tell Mammy"* (emphasis original, Enright 9). In addition, she describes herself and her sibling Liam as their parents' ostracized children:

> I don't know if she would like me better, if she could remember my name. Mammy was always free to choose which ones she did and did not love. The boys first, of course, and after the boys, whichever of the girls were good.
> 
> I was not good. I am not sure why. It is not that I ever did anything out of the way. I just didn't buy it, and neither did Liam. We just didn't buy the whole Hegarty *poor Mammy* thing. (Enright 184)

However, despite the harsh criticism of her mother and grandmother, Veronica feels angry to find out she has so much in common with them: "I am the one who looks most like her own mother, my grandmother Ada. It must be confusing" (Enright 4). As a result of her storytelling, she experiences a shift in her perspective towards her mother by becoming more compassionate and sympathetic. She compares her mother to a "sweet child" (Enright 212), and tries to tell her the truth about what happened to Liam in his childhood; "I am saying that, the year you sent us away, your dead son was interfered with, when you were not there to comfort or protect him, and that interference was enough to send him on a path that ends in the box downstairs. That is what I am saying, if you want to know" (Enright 213). In this way, she also finds her mother to be a victim of what happened in the past, or as a person who terribly suffered from the past events: "the pain of it [the past] belongs to her more than it does to me, I think [...] Maybe she had more past than most people, to wipe clear" (Enright 233). Thus, she experiences a meaningful shift in her perspective towards her mother since, in comparing the impact of her brother's death on herself and on her mother at the beginning part of her remembering series, she belittled her mother's loss: "She would cry no matter what son he was. It occurs to me that we have got something wrong here, because I am the one. She has plenty more" (Enright 11). Thus, her storytelling and acts of remembering help her understand herself and others such as her mother and brother.

Liam's embedded narrative is a significant memory patch in the body of Veronica's entire series of acts of remembering. Through reviewing the available memory pieces related to Liam and through filling in the missing parts by her imaginings, Veronica tries to define her mysterious brother so that she can understand him as well as herself. She is mentally and emotionally caught in the memory of his brother being abused by Lamb Nugent—her grandmother's suitor, friend, and landlord—and what he did to him when he was a little child:

> I cannot move. In this memory or dream, I can neither stop it, nor make it continue. Whatever comes out of his mouth will horrify me, though I know it cannot harm me. It will fill the world but not mark it. It is there already [...]: the feeling that Lamb Nugent is mocking us all; that even the walls are oozing his sly intent. The pattern on the wallpaper repeats to nausea, while hot in my grasp, and straight and, even at this remove of years, lovely, Nugent's wordless thing bucks, proud and weeping in my hand. (Enright 222).

*The Gathering* can be read as the narrator's long obituary about her favourite brother who has recently committed suicide. In other words, Liam lies at the centre of Veronica's childhood experiences and her adulthood storytelling activity. Since, as she claims, of all her family members, she is "the one who loved him [Liam] most" (Enright 11), because he "decided to stay important, to the end" (Enright 28), his death is presented as a turning point in her perspective towards the past—of herself and her brother. Veronica's sense of identity is interwoven with the identity she tries to ascribe to her brother throughout her acts of remembering and her evaluation of them. Thus, she tries to remember her past as she feels obliged to disclose her brother's character as well as the main reason for his suicide. Despite her ambition to have a realistic recollection, she can only recreate what happened to him as well as his identity through her imaginings.

Veronica's main mission as the storyteller is to find out the truth about her brother as she thinks there should be a connection between what happened to him when he was nine years old, and his committing suicide after about twenty years. However, she finds it difficult to do so since neither her brother nor the events related to him are retrievable through her acts of remembering. For example, she cannot "recall Liam in any detail" and cannot "remember Liam's face" (Enright 64 and 65). Therefore, more than remembering her brother, she recreates him through his effects and connections: "There are photographs. There is the hint of my brother's smile in my own mirror, a tone of voice I sometimes hit. I do not think we remember our family in any real sense. We live in them, instead. The only things I am sure of are the things I never saw—my little blasphemies" (Enright 66). Her storytelling, thus, is her fiction of the past rather than documentation of it.

As is generally true about her other embedded narratives in *The Gathering*, Veronica tries to represent the unrepresentable with regard to Liam:

> Liam was always mysteriously elsewhere: this perhaps one of the effects of our stay at Ada's, that if he made a home, it was only ever to leave it. I don't know why I didn't mind: I was jealous of his freedom, certainly, but I think I realised, even then, that the place he went to was always less interesting

> than the one he had left behind, or more terrible. Liam was prone to boredom and decline; he was too vague and restless to make a tragic object of himself, even then. (Enright 121)

Under the impact of his death and in her mourning period for him, Veronica tries to understand the real reasons that brought about his death because, as she contends, the dead needs "The truth. The dead want nothing else. It is the only thing that they require" (Enright 156). The presented version of the truth is, however, a narrative or constructed one. It is mostly based on the unreal events because she tries to recount the unnarratable. Based on ambiguous evidence, Veronica constructs a fictional reality which counts to her as more real than the real one.

In terms of Liam's narrative, Veronica is in control of her fanciful and image-producing mind. Her narrative is, in other words, under the yoke of her creative imagination. For example, although she has never seen her Uncle Brenden in real life, when her sister Kitty gives her the news of his death, Veronica tries to understand him through storying his life and situation so that she might find out her own thoughts and feelings of him:

> I was sure I had never met him, though now here he is, suddenly at the Christmas table in Griffith Way, a face made fantastic by falling jowls, his nostrils rimmed red and his eyes—his eyes when I think of them were tired and unpleasant, as though madness was a tedious business; nearly as tedious as Christmas. My memory puts him in an orange paper hat, with a glass of brandy in his shaking hand, but there was no alcohol in our house until Liam started smuggling it in, and there were no paper hats either. (Enright 156-157)

Veronica's storytelling, thus, includes her feelings of sympathy through which she tries to understand the mental states of the characters as the objects of her story. It enables her to read their minds in accordance with the requirements of her narrative.

Liam's death is presented as an awakening event for Veronica throughout the entire narrative. It encourages her to face the realities of her own past and present lives:

> I thought about this as I sat in the Shelbourne bar—that I was living my life in inverted commas. I could pick up my keys and go 'home' where I could 'have sex' with my 'husband' just like lots of other people did. This is

what I had been doing for years. And I didn't seem to mind the inverted commas, or even notice that I was living in them, until my brother died. (Enright 181)

Veronica's recollection of the scene in which the "terrified" (Enright 146) Liam was subjected to Nugent's sexual harassment reveals how her episodic memory is surrounded by uncertainly:

And even though I know it is *true* that this happened, I do not know if I have the true picture in my mind's eye [...] The image has too much yellow light in it, there are too many long shadows thrown. [...] I think it may be a false memory, because there is a terrible tangle of things that I have to fight through to get to it, in my head. And also because it is unbearable. (Enright 144)

What Veronica dubs as "a false memory" constitutes the fundamental part of her storytelling and acts of remembering. In other words, all her subjective experience in *The Gathering* is about the possible impact of what might happened in this scene regarding Liam's behaviour, life and death. She remembers some details vividly: "I have seen great bleakness in Liam's eyes, on that day and on many days since" (Enright 146). Despite that, she is aware of misremembering an experience from the time when she was just eight years old: "I look at my own children and I think you know everything at eight. But maybe I am wrong. You know everything at eight, but it is hidden from you, sealed up, in a way you have to cut yourself open to find" (Enright 147). Although she is "not sure" (Enright 151) what really happened and how it happened, she arrives at her conclusion based on both remembering and not remembering, or based on what she "assume[s]" (Enright 146) might have happened.

Veronica's mind is haunted by some episodic memories and is it full of Liam's memories, words, and, towards the end of narrative, hallucinations. She feels guilty that despite his will she missed a close connection with him (Enright 126) and thus failed "to save Liam" (Enright 203). Veronica represents Liam's committing suicide as a symbolic act showing "the way we all [the Hegartys] failed" (Enright 203). She interprets it as a revealing moment:

"Something has happened to this family. The knot has come loose" (Enright 210).

Veronica defines Liam as "beyond the rules," "unfit for the adult world" (Enright 163), as an "emigrant brother," "an old-fashioned ghost," who "always seemed a bit of a throwback, a hick" (Enright 191), and as a "guy who stuck around, the one who would not go. He was the guy who could not be relied upon, the messer" (Enright 123). In a conversation with her daughter on Liam's death, Veronica describes Liam as a person who was "sick, in his head" (Enright 175). Liam-related memories help her find her true feelings and thoughts about him as she generally tries to be frank in her embedded narratives:

> Liam never had any truck with self-pity, his own, or anyone else's. When someone was miserable—Kitty, for example—it was always for the wrong reasons as far as he was concerned. Don't get me wrong, Liam loved people who suffered—he loved the poor, the destitute, the lonely, the alcoholic, he pitied anyone with a problem, just so long as they didn't pity themselves. Which doesn't sound altogether fair to me. Which sounds like *pride*, to me. (emphasis original, Enright 167-168)

Comparing Liam to herself, she shares with us her thoughts about him: "I wanted to be a girl. I wanted to have sex that meant something. [...] There was a path, I thought—I really thought that there must be a path—and Liam had wandered off it, and I wasn't going out there to look for him" (Enright 123). Her acts of remembering Liam provide her with an excuse to acquit herself of his blaming:

> I know I sound bitter [...] my brother blamed me for twenty years or more [...] He treated me like I was selling out on something, though on what I do not know—because Liam did not allow dreams either, of course. My brother had strong ideas about justice, but he was unkind to every single person who tried to love him; mostly, and especially, to every woman he ever slept with, and still, after a lifetime of spreading the hurt around, he managed to blame me. And I managed to feel guilty. (Enright 168)

Despite all these, she thinks that "the problem with Liam was never something big. The problem with Liam was always a hundred small things" (Enright 124). She envies him and tries to reveal in her narrative his "great talent," which according to her, was "exposing the lie" (Enright 125). However, she cannot say what exactly made him different: "Liam could be a completely shocking human being, but it was hard to say what exactly he had done to make you feel so off-key" (Enright 125). Although she thinks that his alcoholism "made him vicious" (Enright 125), she knows that it was not, and cannot be, the main cause of his decline and death.

As a result of her storytelling and her incomplete memories Veronica discovers the truth about some fictional characters. As she does so about Ada and Liam, she also arrives at an obvious conclusion about Nugent's character and intentions. The root of his crime, according to her, was his lack of love: "Nugent was just a small-timer; he didn't have much of it [love] to throw around" (Enright 235), and the fact that "children in those days were of little account." Therefore, as Veronica realizes, Nugent's sexual harassment was his proclamation of his desire for "revenge" (Enright 236) for not being loved by his grandmother, Ada. In recounting her memory of Nugent's sexual abuse of Liam, Veronica tries to experience the events through her sympathetic imaginings so that she might reveal the truth regarding what really happened.

The fact that she discovers the truth about Liam through remembering as well as imagining some details about Nugent's abuse of Liam, does not mean that she finally knows everything about Liam and the different aspects of what Nugent did to him on his subsequent life:

> I don't know when Liam's fate was written in his bones. And although Nugent was the first man to put his name there, for some reason, I don't think he was the last. Not because I saw anything else going on, but because this is the way these things work. Of course, no one knew how these things *worked* at the time. We looked at the likes of Liam and had a whole other story for it, a different set of words. (emphasis original, Enright 163)

By the end of her story, Veronica admits that she has still some vague memories about what happened to Liam and to herself in the past. For example, in wondering whether Nugent abused herself too, she comes to some uncertain conclusions, "I add it [the possibility of Nugent's abuse] in to my life, as an event, and I think, well yes, that might explain some things. I add it into my brother's life and it is crucial; it is the place where all cause meets all effect, the crux of the X. In a way, it explains too much" (Enright 224). Therefore, although by relying on the evidence, facts as well as her own imaginings, Veronica finds out some truth about the past, still there are some undiscovered issues:

> These are the things I do, actually know. I know that my brother Liam was sexually abused by Lambert Nugent. Or was probably sexually abused by Lambert Nugent. These are the things I don't know: that I was touched by Lambert Nugent, that my Uncle Brendan was driven mad by him, that my mother was rendered stupid by him, that my Aunt Rose and my sister Kitty got away. In short, I know nothing else about Lambert Nugent; who he was and how Ada met him; what he did, or did not do. (Enright 224)

She ascribes her achievements in narrative to Liam, as the cause of her intention to examine the past and find out the hidden details about a secret: "I owe it to Liam to make things clear — what happened and what did not happen in Broadstone. Because there are effects. We know that. We know that real events have real effects. In a way that unreal events do not" (Enright 223).

Towards the end of her narrative of Liam, Veronica's memory of his character, life, and death gradually fades away. Despite her bitter criticism of Liam, she tries to "cross" his "look" (Enright 172). Her memory of him finally meets his death:

> Liam turns to watch me as I go. He does not know who I am, or what the sea is, or what sort of a place Broadstone might be. He is full of his own death. His death fills him as a plum fills its own skin. Even his eyes are full. It is a serious business, being dead. He would like to do it well. He turns from the confusing lights of the car and sets his face towards the sea. (Enright 239)

At the end of her narration, Veronica accepts Liam's death by what she considers as paying her debt to him through remembering him and examining his life as much as she can. Her storytelling helps her to reveal the truth about what happened to him when he was nine years old, and highlight the impact of the event on his uncommon life and death. Thus, Veronica's storytelling is her effort to overcome a sense of humiliation and "shame" that Liam's suicide has brought to the Hegartys (Enright 168). Through imitating his brother's life, her storytelling is her effort to expose the hypocrisy and lie: "like Liam, I say, 'Pull the whole thing down.' […] As if the world was built on a lie and that lie was very secret and very dirty" (Enright 168). Therefore, her acts of remembering, both based her recollections and construction of memories, help her to redefine the identity of her family and all the people connected to it. Veronica's skill as a storyteller is thus to make a coherent whole out of the seemingly disconnected memory patches. This allows her to overcome her uncertainty about past events and situations and regain her mental and emotional tranquillity at last.

 Regaining a peace of mind is also the main narrative point in Anna Bruns's *Milkman*. As is explored in the next chapter, the unnamed narrator's storytelling is her act of recollecting some historic events she went through roughly two decades before remembering them. In her episodic memories, her survival methods against a suppressive social world are presented as the main causes in bringing about a big turn in her life.

# FOUR
# Mirror of the Past:
# Narrator as Rememberer in Anna Burns's *Milkman*

> "The past was the enemy in Ireland, her papa said another time."
> (William Trevor 10)

The Northern Irish Booker Prize-winning writer Anna Burns's third novel *Milkman* is a long narrative of painful, disturbing, but constructive memories. It depicts the sociocultural problems of being a woman in the traditional and harsh Irish community at the height of the so-called Troubles during the 1970s. Retrospectively and after about two decades, the narrator tries to realistically recount some memories of the terrific situation she experienced in her late adolescent years in an unsettled society. Focalising the narrative through a female character-narrator's perspective, Burns in *Milkman* mainly presents a socio-familial Irish life on the verge of destruction, disintegration, and transformation.

*Milkman* belongs to the Irish tradition of the English-language novel. It shares the ironic tone of the works created by the Irish authors of English literature such as Jonathan Swift, George Bernard Shaw, William Butler Yeats, James Joyce and Samuel Beckett. Reminding us of the stream-of-consciousness technique widely applied by modernist writers, *Milkman* narrates the traumatic experience of a late-adolescent female character. The grown-up narrator narrates her younger self's unresolved conflict with the principles of her family, community and society. Thus, as in *The Sea* and *The Gathering*, the distinguishing factor of the narrator's memories in *Milkman* is the impact of time. However, more than being about the personal side of time, *Milkman* mainly represents the "psycho-political atmosphere" (Burns 24) which imposed stressful experiences and a traumatic life on the narrator.

*Milkman* begins with the narrator's account of her memories. After about two decades, she is remembering her difficult life as a woman in the past. The trace and impact of mental wounds drive her desire to tell her story. Remembering in *Milkman* is a human-like action. It has both personal and social aspects since, as Brady Wagoner contends, "human remembering is both a personal and a social—culturally situated process: It is personal in that it expresses a unique life history and concerns, and it is social—cultural in that it is deeply enmeshed in social relationships and meanings provided by different groups" (4).

*Milkman* is a novel about living with fear and trauma mainly caused by "unspoken rules and regulations" (Burns 22) within the "context" of an "intricately coiled, overly secretive, hyper-gossipy, puritanical yet indecent, totalitarian district" (Burns 172). It is about a polarized society in "those darker of the dark days" when "All ordinary people also understood the basics of what was allowed and not allowed of what was neutral and could be exempted from preferences, from nomenclature, from emblems and from outlooks" (Burns 22). The difficulties of being a woman in a patriarchal society, or the hatred of 1970s, lie at the heart of plot in *Milkman* wherein rumours, gossips, and "tribal identification" (Burns 24) played a destructive role in the narrator's closed community.

*Milkman* is a novel about the experiential memories of an unnamed female citizen in an unnamed setting among unnamed people. Through her acts of remembering, the narrative presents the way its narrator struggled to survive in a trouble-ridden society in the past. In her retellings, she highlights the impact of rumours, gossips, and political violence as the main causes of her intense mental suffering. In other words, on the one hand, *Milkman* is a monograph showing how the narrator once in her life succeeded in overcoming the mental aberrations imposed on her by the dominant and highly divided patriarchal order. On the other hand, the main purpose of acts of remembering in *Milkman* is to evaluate and understand the political, social, and/or cultural issues of the narrator's society two decades before the time of narration.

*Milkman* is, therefore, a novel primarily about the severe psychological bullying that its narrator suffered in her past, roughly two decades before recounting it. Narrated through the perspective of an eighteen-year-old narrator, it traces the mental operation of the narrator's younger self during a troubled time. The retrospective narrative presents the painful impact of surviving in a problematic community in which the narrator felt insecure and under control. The narrative has a circular plotline as it begins with a memory by which it also ends. The grown-up narrator remembers an eventful day on which the Milkman died and one Somebody McSomebody threatened her to death. The whole narrative is narrated under the spell of the factor present in its first sentence—threat. The narrative is based on a duality implied from its beginning—the narrator vs. the dominant social mind. *Milkman* is thus mainly about the threatening effects of a dominant conflict on the narrator's mental state, "The day Somebody McSomebody put a gun to my breast and called me a cat and threatened to shoot me was the same day the milkman died" (Burns 1). By remembering how she faced threat on the part of the two men, the former was a person whom the narrator's mother wanted her to marry and the latter was her troublemaker on the streets, the narrator shares with us the traumatic impact of her younger self's experiences on her mental health and functioning.

*Milkman* is a bildungsroman which represents its narrator's learnings and development. In a retrospective manner, the narrator changes her narration into an act of confession to herself and to the readers. To put it another way, the narrator uses storytelling to examine the mental impacts of some socio-familial events in her past life. She looks into her own mind to follow and study the traces of a traumatic period in her life. This changes into the defining desire in the narrative in a way that leads to the reinvigoration of the already passive reminiscence of the destructive experience in her mind. By focusing on the affective aspects of the protagonist's experience, the narrating act, however, helps the narrator to some extent come to terms with the unresolved effects of her experience.

The manner of the represented storyworld's functioning in *Milkman* is the cardinal source of the conflict around which the narrative spins. Although its representation is not the primary goal of the narrative, the war-ridden setting illustrates an already divided society—between the so-called renouncers and the defenders of the state or between the Irish nationalists and the supporters of the puppet government established by the British Empire. The chaotic atmosphere of the narrator's society facilitates the exploitation of human rights, and above all women's rights. The eponymous Milkman is the prime example of such exploitation. He is one of the leading members of the renouncers in the territory controlled by the revolutionists. His encounter with the narrator, which immediately brings about ever-increasing gossip about their clandestine relationship, leads to her total breakdown, both mentally and socially.

Besides the highly political patriarchal atmosphere, the narrator's family, as an important social institution, is presented as a main source of the mental pain inflicted on her. Her traditional family represents the strict principles of the superstitious and gossip-loving society. Her mother is a woman of rules and duties. She does not tolerate a daughter who rejects marriage and, based on the growing gossip, who has a clandestine relationship with a married older man. Representing the previous generation of female society, her mother marks the central gap within the narrative construction. She considers marriage a holy duty the rules of which every woman should obey. Towards the end of the narrative, the real Milkman, with whom the narrator's mother shares a romantic past, returns to the storyworld, and the mother confesses how her own marriage of duty has in fact been a marriage of failure. She had to live with a husband without loving him. The more the narrator's mother accepts her own mistakes, the more she becomes sympathetic towards her daughter, the narrator.

The narrator's supposed "affair" (Burns 1) with a paramilitary renouncer, referred to at first as milkman and later in the novel as Milkman (with a capital M), feeds the unending and ever-growing rumour about her in a way such that she begins "experiencing [...] under-the-surface turbulence" (Burns 177). The source of this rumour is the narrator's first brother-in-law whose only function in the narrative is to spread rumours about her and the Milkman. Jeopardising her position in the socio-familial system, his "predatory nature" (Burns 2) puts her mental health at great risk. Thus, the narrator recounts how under the effect of the growing rumour concerning the dishonourable relationship between her eighteen-year-old self and the Milkman, she changed into a scarlet letter in her community where the social minds accused her of immorality.

The narrator in *Milkman* is considered a disgrace both to her family and to her community. The sense of being rejected by the socio-communal patriarchal mentality gradually drives the narrator into a mental breakdown. She feels as if she is always under the gaze of the symbolic Milkman. The traumatic effect of this feeling shows its impact throughout her life and relationships. Milkman changes her into a scapegoat. The flood of rumour and gossip regarding their made-up relationship marginalises her and puts her life in serious threat. Milkman's lethal effects on the experiencing self of the narrator continues until he is assassinated by the state men. His death, which is symbolically concurrent with the return to the community of the famous real Milkman, marks the revival of her already deeply damaged feelings and thoughts. Through her intentional act of reconciliation, she helps her mother to confess her true thoughts and feelings and publicly pursues her buried love of the real Milkman. In this way, the narrator is gradually accepted into her own community. Symbolically, she regains her strength through inhaling the "softening" (Burns 348) evening light of her context.

A third brother-in-law, a longest friend, and a maybe-boyfriend are the characters in her community who can to some extent protect the narrator against the rumours. However, the patriarchal order is also present in the relationship between the narrator and them. The thoughtful narrator thinks of her one-year-long relationship with her maybe-boyfriend as a preliminary step before marriage. She experiences a cautious intimacy with him. At the end of the long and destructive effect of Milkman on their relationship, when she finds the true reality of her maybe-boyfriend's character towards the end of the narrative, the significant role of her cautiousness in her behaviour becomes more obvious. In other words, the conservative, circumspect aspect of her character saves her from a possible marriage doomed to failure. Likewise, although her third brother-in-law is a famous supporter and protector of the women in their community, he does not have the capacity to think about their psychological suffering. He can only think of the physical damage a woman might experience in her community. This aspect of his character is portrayed through his interest in doing exercises, in his utmost care for the physical aspects of his body.

How did the narrator come out of all the mess in her community? To put it otherwise, what were her techniques for overcoming a strenuous situation? The answer to such questions is in fact the main concern in the plotline for the erudite narrator and possibly for the author herself. After about two decades, the narrator, now in her forties, is contemplating the way she could survive the difficult moment in her life. In other words, she re-evaluates the destructive events and situation she experienced at the onset of 1970s when Women's Issues were not considered or recognized as issues at all. After two decades of the horrific and traumatic experience, the narrator explores the ways through which she could survive such an unsafe society via "dissembling and use of face" (Burns 176). Thus, she tries to show us how through creating and protecting an inner self, which required her wearing a social mask, she could overcome the psycho-physical burden of an oppressive environment since her "real [self] was in there, in charge, hidden from them but directing from the undergrowth" (Burns 176).

Two-voicedness, thus, is an embedded part of Burns's narrative. She shows us the conflict between the narrator's true self (voice) and the consciously constructed, or made-up one. This is a self-invented method that the narrator's self-conscious mind came up with as the only effective solution for the problem. Hence, the narrator is presented as the only self-conscious character in the storyworld. Her sympathetic mind ponders the main issues and the other characters' thoughts and (re)actions in her story. In her acts of remembering, she decodes the way her community and the social minds in it functioned, through presenting a fake self, a false face, or a version of herself which did not let the others to get into her true thoughts and emotions. She wore a mask in order to protect her true self. The more she did so the more she enlarged her inner capacity, or her toleration level. This was her only self-curing method. Through her method, she could empower the rational side of her mind which enabled her to analyse all her actions and behaviour in a logical way and to stay safe in an age of division.

The narrator in *Milkman* is a person interested in fictional narrative. She is a devout reader of fiction. When the Milkman sees her for the first time, she is reading *Ivanhoe*. She talks to her maybe-boyfriend about such great narratives as *The Brothers Karamazov*, *Tristram Shandy*, *Vanity Fair* and *Madame Bovary*. Her imaginative mind helps her to live in a world beyond its current issues. Reading fiction helped her to alienate herself from her undesirable context. Besides regaining her social status, the narrator's unique and hard-to-read method also prevented the breakdown of her family. She knowingly tried not to make the mistakes the previous generation of women in her society had made. She finally understood that her mother's arrogant reaction towards her mostly supposed, imagined, or fabricated actions stemmed from her own psychological problems which had roots in her dark past. Her unwilling confession of failure in love and marriage initiated an already missing mother-daughter sympathetic bond between the two. The reconciliation at home brings about the desired safety for the narrator in the storyworld at the end.

Highlighting a female citizen's experience during the Troubles in 1970s Belfast is a thread woven through the critical reactions to *Milkman*. It is, according to Margarita Estevez Saa, "a brilliant representation of the extraordinary powers of perception of a young female character" (89). Studying it from "a narrative perspective," Clare Hutton holds that "*Milkman* blends passages of memory, thought, and apparently random associations with a more conventional first-person narration, focused on telling the story of what happened to 'middle sister' during the few months in 1979 when she was stalked" (359). According to Maria-Adriana Deina, the narrator-character keeps us engaged through remembering, retelling, and representation of her "thoughts, feelings and dilemmas as suspicion and gossip about her affair with the dangerous man begin to circulate in her community, drawing social pressure and unwanted attention in the backdrop of protracted violence and the dark days of the Troubles." In other words, "The novel is both deeply steeped in the specific historicity of the Troubles, while also narrating experiences that are irreducible to this context" (30). Similarly, Beata

Piątek also highlights the superiority of the narrator's personal "experience" to the issue of "historical truth" in Burns's narrative by arguing that "it [*Milkman*] is remarkable, not so much for revealing the historical truth about the experience of young women growing up in the Troubles, but for developing the author's own form of language, of a traumatic realism, to communicate this experience with a poignancy which is beyond the reach of any historical account" (107). Leszek Drong is one of the few critics who has rightly highlighted the centrality of memory in *Milkman* by contending that in this novel "what comes to fore .... is the work of (and the reliability) of memory" (172). Analysing the narrative through the lens of transcultural memory, Drong argues that in *Milkman* "what is undoubtedly fascinating is how the individual memory of the narrators is implicated in the collective memory of their communities" (172). The private or individual memory of the narrator is also analysed in the following parts of this chapter as a salient narrative element in *Milkman*. The main contention of this chapter is that the narrator's storytelling, which is driven by her acts of remembering, is a re-experiencing and imagining process of an unsettling experience. In her story, the narrator presents herself as a victim of abuse in the past. From this perspective, *Milkman* belongs to the canon of contemporary Irish fiction since "representation of an abused subjectivity," according to Eva Patten, is one of the characteristics of contemporary Irish fiction:

> In fiction, the impact of women writing is marked in narrative modes geared to the representation of an abused subjectivity. Several authors use autobiographical or Bildungsroman constructions to depict the individual as the victim of serial political, religious and cultural restrictions in Ireland [...] From the mid 1980s onwards, the prevalence of first-person and rites-of-passage narratives projecting the plight of female protagonists amounted to a sustained fictional campaign of self-assertion. The novel has been a means by which a marginalised female voice claimed authority in response to the ingrained misogyny of Irish life. (268-269)

The female narrator presents a repressed version of her voice in the story time. Her storytelling is an account of her memories of abused subjectivity that focuses on their effects which are still lingering in her mind. Storytelling, therefore, is a self-made remedy for the narrator's emotional suffering.

Made up of seven parts, *Milkman* has a nonlinear plotline. The narrator-character recounts her account of different achronological events from various times in her past life. Unlike the highly personal or private point of narration in *The Sea* and *The Gathering*, the main narrative point in *Milkman* is the classical dichotomy of self and society. The mature narrator's episodic memories are her unique documents and evidence from a harsh and unkind society towards an innocent young woman in a transforming time. She tells her story to alleviate the burden of her suffering caused by the defining factors of her time such as the political situation, tradition, and gender. Her memories are mainly about her survival techniques in a highly problematic context. Her remembering is a self-reminding act. She reminds herself of her ability and skill in overcoming the debilitating problems of her society.

The narrator's memories most often bring about evaluation of her thoughts and behaviour in the past as she constantly makes comments on her previous thoughts and actions. For example, having admitted her insufficient knowledge about sex when she was eighteen, "At eighteen … I was never going to admit that, regarding sex, there was an awful lot I didn't understand about it" (Burns 127), she criticises her society for not allowing her to do so: "Surely at eighteen, I ought to have been allowed to think for a little longer that I did" (Burns 128). In this way, she represents herself as a shrewd woman of deep knowledge of herself and of others, a person aware of the impact of her words and behaviour on other people's thoughts and behaviours. By trying to read people's thoughts and intentions, she used to talk as much as she remained silent. For example, when she was talking with Somebody McSomebody, as she remembers, she "decided not to cut in to correct, for that would encourage him [McSomebody] on" (Burns 131). This strategy of being and seeming "polite" (Burns 132) made her survival possible in her dangerous society. Likewise, her seeming mindreading ability enabled her to control other people's behaviour. She was an acute observer of people and context as she succeeded in protecting herself, and "refused to be evoked, drawn out, shocked into revelation" (Burns 174) by the help of her "verbal defence repertoire" in which "'*I don't know*' [was] the biggest player," or by her "suspiciousness of questions," her "learning," and "feigned emotions" (Burns 174, 172, 241 and 301).

The final part of the novel can be considered as a space of revival, recovery, regeneration, and "revolution[s]" (Burns 333). At the end of our companionship with the narrator's tortuous act of mental travelling, we finally share her sense of relief and being "pleased" (Burns 340). We share her feeling of joy and refreshment revealed through the shift in the narrative mode and tone. We also get to know the main reasons behind her desire to recount the memories of some painful experiences. The fact that her two-month-lasting experience of imperilment and "mental wreckage" (Burns 347) finally ends in a family reunion and personal recovery is represented as a hilarious experience to the remembering narrator as much as to her audience too. She remembers how she regained a new sense of awareness: "I inhaled the early evening light and realised this was softening, [...] I exhaled this light and for a moment, just a moment, I almost nearly laughed" (Burns 348). Thus, on the verge of her forties, the narrator proudly remembers the most difficult time in whole her life when, despite the context, she could find ways to protect herself, and survive traumatic moments.

The narrator's act of remembering in *Milkman* is her way to forget a significant period in her life in a similar way to how she decided to do so after the Milkman's death: "Whatever he had been and whatever he'd been called, he was gone, so I did what usually I did around death which was to forget all about it" (Burns 305). As is shown in the next parts, five "irreconcilables" "dominated" the narrator's "mind" in the time of story: maybe-boyfriend, their 'not quite on, not quite off' relationship, Milkman, the renouncers, and political problems (Burns 113). The narrator's acts of remembering, therefore, include her memories as well as her evaluation of them after about two decades.

## 4.1 Remembering as a Reliable Medium of Retelling (History)

*Milkman* is a realistic historical narrative in which remembering is presented as a reliable medium of narration. Unlike the uncertain nature of memory and acts of remembering in *The Sea* and *The Gathering*, reliability is not a point of concern for the narrator in *Milkman*. By retrieving the details from her memory, the narrator, on the one hand, relates the main socio-historical events in her story, and, on the other hand, she presents a process of development in her sense of identity through time.

The setting in *Milkman* has a paramount importance in the construction of narrative. *Milkman* can be read as the narrator's epic about a "trophy time" of "trauma" and "darkness" (Burns 29 and 115), a time in which the "the spirit of the community [was] going back in time" (Burns 22), and the ready possibility of being named a "traitor" (Burns 27) was a live threat to everyone. The narrator ascribes the root of the socio-political problems she suffered in the past to the historical period: "These were knife-edge times, primal times, with everybody suspicious of everybody" (Burns 27). Moreover, *Milkman* is about "being judged in […] turbulent times", about "bigotry", "prejudice", "exclusion," and "revenge" (Burns 28 and 29), about "the era of not letting bygones be bygones" (Burns 25). The narrator portrays the dominance of these characteristics with the example of a supercharger gained by her maybe-boyfriend by showing how his community accused him of owning something belonging to those living on the other side of the road. She highlights their "ambivalent look" (Burns 33). The remembered time was a moment of "Sectarianism" (Burns 115) as well as a time of crushing communal hatred, or in the narrator's words, "the great Seventies hatred" which was beyond "the misleading and cumbersome inadequacy of the political problems, and all rationalisations and choice conclusions about the political problems" (Burns 96).

*Milkman* is a representation of an environment "overwhelmingly consisting of fear and of sorrow" (Burns 90). It condemns the narrator's society in a particular time of fragmentation, a time in which reading minds was a common strategy used by people "in order to protect themselves, they could also, at certain moments when they knew their mind was being read, learn to present their topmost mental level to those who were reading it whilst in the undergrowth of their consciousness, inform themselves privately of what their true thinking was about" (Burns 36-37). Furthermore, it is a narrative about a time in which shame "hadn't yet entered the communal vocabulary." Although everybody was familiar with "the feeling of shame," or it "was a public feeling," nobody wanted to have it. Rather, they went through "all kinds of permutations in order not to have it: killing people, doing verbal damage to people, doing mental damage to people and, not least, also not infrequently, doing those things to oneself" (Burns 53). In the same way, "moods" was a term used for "depressions" since at that time the latter term did not exist (Burns 85).

*Milkman* is a sad narrative of pain and suffering. The grown-up narrator remembers some episodes from her difficult time in the past. Although the events she went through happened in a short time in her late adolescent life, they had a long and deep impact on her mind. Thus, by remembering her fearful and constantly threatened life in the past, the narrator indirectly celebrates the freedom she has had after that time.

Through her episodic memories, the narrator in *Milkman* re-experiences some of the humiliating, agonizing, and distressful moments in her past. The main goal of her acts of remembering, however, is beyond pain. Rather, in her long contemplation, the narrator tries to understand her past life through her adult mind as much as she aims to show how time in the past was different from the present. Her story includes some embedded narratives which advance through the overall narrative plot—her supposed relationship with an intruder called Milkman, her story of her transforming relationship with her mother, and her stormy relationship with her maybe-boyfriend are the main sub-narratives which all in all constitute the overall plot in *Milkman*.

*Milkman* is also about a time when it was "impossible" to be neutral since "a person could not help but have a view" (Burns 112). The public or social mind of the time had its own classification of "mental aberrations: the slight, communally accepted ones and the not-so-slight, beyond-the-pale ones. Those possessing the former fitted tolerably into society and this was pretty much everybody, including all the various drinkers, fighters and rioters who existed in this place" (Burns 59). In the same way, the duality extended to the animals as the cats were hated, with the narrator called a cat in the storyworld, while the dogs were favoured since they "were sturdy, loyal, feudal, good for man's account of himself and with a slavish need to be obedient to someone" (Burns 94). Although the narrator was "conditioned […] by those times, by a learned revulsion" (Burns 94), since she resisted such classifications, she had problems.

It is the story of a community where people are caught between two dangerous forces — the separatists and the police, or the state representatives. It is a narration of darkness and narrow-minded society. Besides, there was no agreement among the existing views as "each was intolerant of the other to the extent that highly volatile, built-up contentions periodically would result from them" (Burns 112). Living in such a community required a special skill: "you had to have manners and exercise politeness to overcome, or at any rate balance out, the violence, the hatred and the blaming — for how to live otherwise?" (Burns 112) It was so because in the community "there was that lack of listening, a stubbornness unyielding, an entrenchment indicative of those turbulent times themselves" (Burns 113).

Set in 1970s Belfast, *Milkman* should not be considered a novel about the political turmoil of the Northern Ireland at that time. Rather, it is mainly about the narrator-character's memories of her experiences when she was on the verge of adulthood. At the time of narration, the narrator is about thirty-eight years old. She tells us what happened when she was eighteen years old. The main point in her acts of remembering is how she dealt with her fear of the Other, or managed her anxiety of being under the gaze of the Other. Her memories are about a time when she was living with a constant feeling of fear and unreliability and was under the control of her family, community, and state. She shares with us the untold story of her tragic life so that she might get rid of the mental impact of the experiences.

The grown-up narrator presents her younger self's ignorance about the realities of her time and place mainly through her interactions with her third brother-in-law, her longest-term friend, mother, and maybe-boyfriend. What the narrator admits in her acts of remembering about her past behaviour and what she recounts as the realities of her community in the past were in fact told to her by her close friend. We learn some important facts about the narrator's character and her situation form the dialogue she remembers she had with her "only [friend] left ... the one person I could speak with, the one person I could listen to, [...] the last trusted-fewest person who wouldn't drain the life out of me that I had left in the world. Like third brother-in-law, she didn't gossip" (Burns 195-196).

The narrator "liked" her third brother-in-law as he was one of the few people in her community who "never gossiped, never came out with lewd remarks or sexual sneers or sneers about anything" (Burns 11). She remembers how she used to hide behind the power of her third brother-in-law against her sense of insecurity and unsafety imposed on her by her gossip-generating society represented by her first brother-in-law. Furthermore, he "paid no attention either to osmosis, to the very noticeable social and political upheaval of the time and the place he was living in. Instead he went about blinkered, unaware, which was weird, very weird. I too, found it weird" (Burns 59). He was considered by women in the neighbourhood as a "champion" (Burns 12). He did not spread gossip and "hadn't been listening to rumour which was in accordance with my respectful view of him as someone with no inclination for rumour" (Burns 63). The narrator "felt safe with him" since he did not "harangue and meddle with who [she] was" (Burns 67). After being two times harassed by Milkman on the street, she chooses to go on running with her third brother-in-law as a part of her hidden agenda or strategy: "I could carry on as if this milkman and our two earlier encounters had been insignificant, or even that they hadn't taken place at all" (Burns 65).

In a similar way to her relationship with her third brother-in-law, the narrator's relationship with her "longest friend" (Burns 203) is at first based on an "unspoken," mutual "agreement" (Burns

202) or understanding, "between us there was an unspoken understanding that I did not ask her her business and in return she did not tell me it" (Burns 197). When the narrator tells her close friend her story with Milkman she feels "relief" (Burns 197).

The reasons for their meeting, as the longest friend utters, is to discuss her "reading-while-walking, […her] unreachable stubbornness at back of it, plus the dangers inherent in it" (Burns 203). Her friend reminds her that as a result of "confounding the community," she has "fallen into the difficult zone" (Burns 204), and the social or communal mind "sees" her as "haughty" (Burns 204). In this way, her old friend puts the mirror in front of the narrator to remind her of her status in their community, from the perspective of the social mind or mass consciousness: "you're considered a community beyond-the-pale" (Burns 199). Her close friend tries to reconcile her with their community by teaching to her the socio-cultural codes, represented by the "unstoppable gossip" (Burns 196). She asks her to "kill out that habit you insist on and that now I suspect you're addicted to—that reading in public as you're walking about" since "The community has pronounced its diagnosis on" her (Burns 200). In this way, her close friend tries to encourage her to "get into proper reality" (Burns 219) through adding to her ongoing "education on just how much I was impacting people without any awareness I'd been visible to people" (Burns 200). The longest friend thus recommends her to turn away from the evil and do the good the things in order to satisfy her community:

> 'Use your loaf, stop the stubbornness, work on your disposition, get off your high horse and show some friendly stray bits. Just something unimportant that would satisfy them rather than encourage them with silence. Then, if you also stop that unfathomable reading-while-walking, that should ameliorate the situation as well.' (Burns 205)

Thus, despite their sympathetic approach to each other at the beginning of their meeting, the narrator loses her "trust" (Burns 203) in her friend as she finds out that her longest friend also repeats the prevalent gossip about her in a way that she must "persuade and prove credible to someone who'd always been in [her] confidence"

(Burns 202). All of a sudden, she stops talking by putting to work her strategy of being silent:

> I needed my silence, my unaccommodation, to shield me from pawing and from molestation by questions. In contrast to friend, I myself was of the view that trying to placate with information to win them over, would not bring benefits of desistence but would encourage and lead them on even more. Besides, I didn't want to. Still I didn't want to. This was my one bit of power in this disempowering world. (Burns 205)

However, before departing, her longest friend advises her about the wide rift between her behaviour and the socio-cultural reality, "The disconnect you have going between your brain and what's out there. This mental misfiring—it's not normal. It's abnormal—the recognising, the not recognising, the remembering, the not remembering, the refusing to admit to the obvious" (Burns 207). The narrator's friend tries to motivate her to stop being non-conformist and refractory since such qualities were considered "mental misfiring" by the social minds. Thus, although her friend acts like a mirror showing her weaknesses, talking to her, and telling her real story about the gossip to some extent relieves the psychological pressure upon her.

Besides her longest friend, the narrator's mother also tries to warn her against the social threats she could face in their community. Memories related to mothers constitute a main part of the narrators' acts of remembering in *The Sea*, *The Gathering*, and *Milkman*. As an important embedded narrative, the narrator's memories with her mother in Burns's narrative move from a negative atmosphere to a positive one. Before their reconciliation towards the end of narrative, they had a troubled relationship for a long time in a way that they "always […] were in fights, always making attack on each other" (Burns 57), and "always […] were at cross purposes" (Burns 224). In her memories, the narrator is mostly caught by her intermittent conversations with her mother, or more precisely by her mother's monologues to her, above all about the necessity of marriage.

In the early parts of her narrative, the narrator describes her mother as a widow who never "budge[d] from" her "position[s]" (Burns 50). For a considerable amount of time, there was no agreement and understanding between the two: "never had it been in my remit not to withhold from my mother because never had it been in her remit to get my message and to take me at my word" (Burns 51). The narrator remembers her mother "upbraid[ing]" her, "harangu[ing] her, and "command[ing]" her to be "a proper girl, a normal girl, a girl with morals intact and a sensibility attuned to what's civilised and respectful" (Burns 121 and 122). Her mother's ignorance of human psychology and relationships represent that of the community. She is represented as having no sense of the psychological problems of her daughter, her "depressions" (Burns 86). As she belonged to a different time, "she was still in her day with her people, not realising it was now my day with different people" (Burns 306). She was a superstitious person. Based on "all the local general gossips" (Burns 48), she tried to persuade her daughter, the narrator, not to marry the Milkman as he was a married, older man, and had a wrong religion. Above all, she continuously reminded her of her "female destiny" (Burns 50).

The narrator's approach to her mother's "haranguing and prolonged mental battering of" her (Burns 53) was to rely on her "defensive, protective, 'giving nothing away' mode" (Burns 51). Her mother strongly believes that she "debased" her parents (Burns 56) by her relationship with the notorious Milkman. Her thoughts in this case were moulded by the communal rumours which made her "anxious" (Burns 45). She interrogated her daughter based on the gossip by saying, "'Your sister says her husband says that he heard everybody else say that you—'" (Burns 51). By her "insulting and disdaining" words (Burns 124), she commands her daughter to behave like a conventional young woman:

> There's nothing wrong with being ordinary, with marrying an ordinary man, with carrying out life's ordinary duties. But I see you're hypnotised by the flashiness, blinded by the ornament, by money, by subcultures, by being taken in, by your very own youth, your immaturity. But it'll end badly [...] You'll come a shell, moulded by him, controlled by him, emptied, leached of all your strength and your animating spirit. You'll be lost, will lose yourself, will slide down into evil. (Burns 123-124)

Having told her mother the real story of her supposed relationship with the Milkman by highlighting that what she heard about it was because of "the twisting of words, the fabrication of words and the exaggeration of words" in their community (Burns 54), the narrator also tells her why she did not take any action against the rumour as she did not want to lose her "power" by trying "to explain and to win over all those gossiping about" herself (Burns 54), "So I'd kept silent, I said. I'd asked no questions, answered no questions, gave no confirmation, no refutation. That way, I said, I'd hoped to maintain a border to keep my mind separate. That way, I said, I'd hoped to ground and protect myself" (Burns 54). At the end of her frank account, her mother calls her "a liar" since in this case "The community was keeping her abreast" (Burns 55). She also accuses her of being "a paramilitary groupie" (Burns 121).

As a highly religious, traditionalist and superstitious person, the narrator's mother thought her daughter(s) should marry, and marry with the right people: "why wasn't I married? This non-wedlock was selfish, disturbing of the God-given order and unsettling for the younger girls, she said" (Burns 45). The driving rule in the narrator's community is to obey the social norms and conventions. She lives in a society in which marriage, together with religion, has a paramount importance. Her three brothers and two elder sisters are married. Her mother saw her as an example to her three daughters of seven, eight, and nine years old. Thus, she gave long sermons on marriage to the narrator as she thought that it was a divine order:

> Marriage wasn't meant to be a bed of roses. It was a divine decree, a communal duty, a responsibility, it was acting your age, having right-religion babies and obligations and limitations and restrictions and hindrances. It was not failing to be proposed to then ending up, yellowed and desiccated, dying some timid but determined spinster on some long-forgotten, dusty, spidery shelf. (Burns 50)

Her mother's mind functioned based on a socio-culturally prescribed "hierarchy" (Burns 85) and duality. For example, her "understanding of the nice wee boys was that they were the right religion, that they were devout, single, preferably not paramilitaries, overall more stable and durable than those—as she put it—'fast, breathtaking, fantastically exhilarating, but all the same, daughter, early-to-death rebel men'" (Burns 50). Her perspective towards the people with depression was also a product of her bilateral mind: "Ma herself didn't get depressions, didn't either, tolerate depressions and, as with lots of people here who didn't get them and didn't tolerate them, she wanted to shake those who did until they caught themselves on" (Burns 85). She also criticized her late husband by "not forgiving him for many things" (Burns 92), based on her dividing mentality by arguing that he was "crazy," soaked in "the political problems" (Burns 86), "despair," and "melancholy" (Burns 87).

Her perspective towards her husband was also under the control of her highly stratified mentality. Since she could not accept the fact that a man could be depressed and/or be taken to a mental hospital, and "under emotional pressure, under peer pressure, shame pressure," she presented "her [unreal or fabricated] take on da's illness to the neighbours" (Burns 91-92). She did so because at that time "even more shame [was] in his case because he was a man. Males and mental hospitals went together far less than females and mental hospitals went together. In a man's case, this equalled a gender falling down in pursuance of his duties, totalling a failure above all to keep face" (Burns 91). All in all, while she presents her mother as an optimist who held a relative perspective towards life and was a socially active person, she also describes her mother as a pessimistic perfectionist who had an intentionally secluded life. They both lacked "a constant goodwill and a trust in people and in life even" (Burns 88).

Being poisoned by someone referred to as Tablets Girl brings about a big change in the plot, in the narrator's relationship with her mother, and in her life. Although her mother at first falsely blames her for becoming pregnant by the Milkman, a revival of mutual empathic feeling between the two grows from this moment on. During her illness, she "did attempt because in that moment, which was a lonely moment, more than ever I longed for her belief in me, for her properly to perceive me" (Burns 224). Her prolonged desire is finally fulfilled as her mother's mind begins "unravelling" (Burns 251) her closely guarded secret—her love of the real Milkman whom her mother could not marry because of the "political situation," "social stigma," the necessity of being "fit [to]convention," "fear of oneself, of one's independence, of one's potential," and "not going for the one you want because by doing so, you might cause envy and anger to arise in others" (Burns 255). At the end of her mother's confession of unfulfilled love for the real Milkman, and having perceived that "da had been the wrong spouse" since her mother had "been in love, still was in love, with real milkman all the time" (Burns 256), the narrator repeats to herself, and to the readers, her account, the reasons she "protected herself" by not marrying because "marrying in doubt, marrying in guilt, marrying in regret, in fear, in despair, in blame, also in terrible self-sacrifice was pretty much the unspoken matrimonial requisite here" (Burns 256). Therefore, as a result of her mother's sincere confession, the narrator encourages her to express her love to the real Milkman publicly. She even tells her lies as she senses that her now aged mother "needed bolstering." Therefore, she "bolstered her with lies which, when all the facts were in, might not have been lies really" (Burns 332). Her mother's reunification with the real Milkman is symbolically a marker of restoring the desired order to the storyworld as finally the foul is punished, and the fair is rewarded. Thus, restoration of love is presented, both in her memories and in her acts of remembering, as equal with happiness, and a peaceful order of life.

As she does from her longest friend and mother, the narrator learns protective and safety lessons from her experience with maybe-boyfriend with whom she spent more time than any other character. She remembers maybe-boyfriend as a non-conformist, an obsessed hoarder of used cars. She remembers how she tried to make him understand that sometimes some things are more important than the others. By narrating the nature of their relationship, the narrator shares with us how she tried to control the operation of her own mind regarding her thoughts and feelings towards her maybe-boyfriend, as she did in her other relationships:

> Secretly I had a worry that maybeboyfriend might not be a proper man. This thought came in the darker moments, in my complex, unbidden moments, swiftly coming, swiftly going and which I wouldn't admit—especially to myself—to having had. If I did, I sensed further contraries would come in its wake because already I'd feel them gathering—to confront me, to throw

off-kilter my certainties. Along with everybody, I dealt with these inner contradictions by turning from them whenever they appeared on the horizon. (Burns 44)

The reason she was attracted to her maybe-boyfriend was the safety zone of in-betweenness he symbolized for her:

> Curious and engaged and eager — because of passion, because of plans, because of hope, because of me. And that was it. With me too, he was uncalculated, transparent, free from deception, always was what he was, with none of that coolness, that withholding, that design, those hurtful, sometimes clever, always mean, manipulations. No conniving. No games-playing. He didn't do it, didn't care for it, had no interest in it. … Uncorrupted in the little things. (Burns 18)

Maybe-boyfriend had a lot in common with the narrator. He offered her what she desired to have in her conservative community. He "always had new things about him, things I hadn't noticed in others, not just in boys before" (Burns 44).

As she does in her narration of different embedded narratives, the narrator presents herself as a character with a high degree of awareness and self-protection in her acts of remembering related to maybe-boyfriend. She knows how to control her thoughts and behaviour at different situations. When her maybe-boyfriend proposes that she "move in with him," before saying "why that [his offer] might not be feasible," she calculates his offer from three different perspectives — her family condition, the nature and quality of her relationship with maybe-boyfriend, and their socio-cultural context (Burns 37). After delving into this issue more, she counts her "reservation" (Burns 43) as the most important reason for not moving in with her maybe-boyfriend as well as for not sharing her problems with him (Burns 280). Moreover, by keeping her relationship in the "maybe" category, she justifies her reservedness towards him by arguing "why would maybe-boyfriend in our maybe-relationship want to know, or think either of us should presume permission to disclose, thoughts, feelings and neediness about that?" (Burns 246).

Milkman's "intimations" (Burns 111) indirectly destroys the "loose status" (Burns 169) of her maybe-relationship with her boyfriend too:

> Before the milkman, maybe-boyfriend's touch, those fingers, his hands, had been the best, the most, the absolute of lovely. But now, since the milkman, any part of maybe-boyfriend coming towards me brought up in me mounting bouts of revulsion and a feeling that I might at any moment be sick. He was repulsing me, my own maybe-boyfriend was repulsing me. (Burns 171)

Her maybe-boyfriend teaches her some lessons about herself, himself, and their community. In his words, she "was no longer a living person but one of those jointed wooden dollies that artists use in—" (Burns 193). She increasingly becomes aware of the similarities between her maybe-boyfriend and the Milkman as she realizes their shared desire to seek domination over her. She becomes aware of his intention to not "further it [their maybe-relationship] into a loving, intimate proper relationship but into one of those stalking, possessive, controlling relationships" (Burns 194). Accordingly, she sees no difference between her maybe-boyfriend and the Milkman, "Then I'd think, he's turning into the Milkman, he's bossing me about, he's thinking he can control me, or else I'd think, he's saying he's had enough of me, so he's taking me home because he wants rid of me [...] he was trying to lame me, to fell me, to cripple me, just like the milkman" (Burns 194). Her fixed character trait was "not to reveal anything" (Burns 195).

The strictness of her mother also had a big impact on the manner of her relationship with her maybe-boyfriend. When he complains that she does not want him to call her directly or to come to her neighbourhood, she says she wants to be "evasive" but does not tell him her reasons:

> I didn't want him calling to the door because of ma. It would have been questions. Then the marriage sermon. Then the baby sermon and, if not them, he'd get accused of being the milkman. Also there were those prayers she'd burst into at any moment, meaning there was just so much discomfiture I could take. So it wasn't shame of him, or to spare him, that we kept things convoluted and parlous by meeting at that dark and bitter sectarian flashpoint. It was to save me the awkwardness of having to explain her. (Burns 74)

The narrator's relationship with her maybe-boyfriend was also shaped by rumours too. The communal opinion about her maybe-boyfriend's supercharger, which was believed to have the flag of the other side on it, and her relationship with the Milkman affected their relationship deeply: "Conjointly, these rumours and their effects upon us were turning bad also for our maybe-relationship" (Burns 189). In her recollection, she sympathises with maybe-boyfriend as she discovers that his strategy against the rumour was similar to her own strategy:

> [I]t was clear to me, that as well as my not telling him about the milkman and the stories doing the rounds in my community about me and the milkman, maybeboyfriend had his own defensive front of silence, stemming from his stubbornness against me and against everybody, as his own way of shielding and keeping safe himself. (Burns 189)

Regarding their relationship, the rumours sometimes govern her mental operation too. For example, when in their conversation on the phone her maybe-boyfriend suggests he go to her house, before giving any answer, she reviews in her mind the possible rumours which would spread by his coming:

> I knew it was unbelievable that I should let myself get pushed into becoming what the gossips were saying I'd already become but, according to the latest in the area, it was the case I'd been in relationship with Milkman for two months by now. That meant it was time to cheat on him, they said, so I was cheating on him, having a dalliance behind his back with some young car mechanic whippersnapper from across town. (Burns 281-282)

The more their conversation continues, the more their dialogue enters some disputed subjects — the narrator's supposed relationship with the paramilitary Milkman and the maybe-boyfriend's possession of a supercharger with the flag on it from the country over the water. So, they decry each other's "insufficiencies" (Burns 286). She feels that maybe-boyfriend became "more and more Milkman" (Burns 283). He marks her reading-while-walking as "'odd, […] Not normal. Not self-preservation. Instead it's unyielding and confounding and in our type of environment it presents you as a stubborn, perverse character'" (Burns 286). Similarly, he makes sarcastic comments about her own character too: "'you don't seem alive anymore. I look at your face and it's as if your sense organs are disappearing or as if they've already disappeared so that no one gets to connect with you. Always you've been hard to second-guess, but now you're impossible. Perhaps we should stop now though, before this gets even worse'" (Burns 286). However, having "decried each other's insufficiencies" (Burns 286), as her "new spontaneity again began to stir itself," she persuades herself to go to maybe-boyfriend and "get this mess cleared up" (Burns 287).

What the narrator sees at maybe-boyfriend's home is the main point in her embedded narrative of him. She gets a "shock" when noticing the existence of a "love" (Burns 230) between her maybe-boyfriend and the chef at his home. By listening at the door to the injured maybe-boyfriend's conversation with his chef, she finds out the secret between the two and the fact that maybe-boyfriend calls her a "wrong person" (Burns 294). As a result of such an awakening experience, she is self-critical:

> What an idiot me, I thought, and I meant in thinking I'd protected myself, believing myself safe from the wrong-spouse category by staying in the maybe-category when it now turns out a person can be done to death in the maybe-category as well. The truth was dawning on me of how terrifying it was not to be numb, but to be aware, to have facts, retain facts, be present, be adult. It was while in the middle of maybe-boyfriend's continued declaration of being an idiot and of my berating myself also for being an idiot, that chef returned the three of us to the moment by demanding the hospital once more. (Burns 294-295)

Having had an eye-opening experience, the narrator's feeling of anger at maybe-boyfriend, the chef, her first brother-in-law, the gossips, and the sycophants disappear. In other words, all of a sudden, she stops feeling angry at the outside world as she becomes aware of her own responsibility in her own situation:

> [I]t was as if I had no right to be angry because if I'd managed this differently it wouldn't now be my fault. If only I'd done such and such instead of such and such, gone there instead of there, said that and not that, or looked different, or hadn't gone out that day with Ivanhoe or that night or that week or anytime during the last two months when I'd let him catch sight of me and want me. (Burns 297)

This experience brings about a big change in the narrator's life. She returns to her family and resumes her ordinary life in a short time. However, she experiences a difficult time throughout her long struggle against the social mind's stubbornness in its restrictive definition of her identity.

## 4.2 The Unnamed Rememberer's Struggle against the Social Mind's Definition of Her Identity

The social mind plays a defining role in the storyworld in *Milkman* and in its narrative construction. The cognitive narratologist Alan Palmer defines social mind as "those aspects of the whole mind that are revealed through the externalist perspective" to mind (39). An externalist approach or perspective towards (fictional) mind, "stresses those aspects that are outer, active, public, social, behavioral, evident, embodied, and engaged" (Palmer 39). Unlike a single consciousness, social mind is "a collective state of mind and group mentality" (Schmid 51). Palmer also argues that "an important part of the social mind is our capacity for intermental thought. Such thinking is joint, group, shared, or collective" (41). Intermental thought is "independent of the individual" thoughts that make it up (Palmer 44). The narrator in *Milkman* shows how the social mind spreads and maintains a collective intermental thought towards her through circulating rumours and gossip, and in this way aims to formulate her identity based on the established social, cultural, and political order.

The social mind plays a fundamental role in *Milkman*. In her memories and acts of remembering, the narrator highlights the public opinion's creative imaginings. More than being affected by Milkman himself, the narrator was affected by the communal representation of her relationship with him. Her storytelling mainly focuses on the difficult time imposed on her by the social mind presented as a dominant element in the fictional community. Everything in the storyworld is filtered through the lens of a social mind. It acted as a main trigger of trauma and mental breakdown for the narrator. It has a gendered structure, and mainly functions based on gossip and rumour. The judgemental nature of this social mind is repressive, restrictive, and threatening. Although it is a communal property, the social mind in *Milkman* has a few active agents.

The narrator's first bother-in-law and Milkman are two characters through whom the basic properties of the social mind are revealed. In her acts of remembering, the narrator refers to the people in her community as a unified body which functioned harmoniously under the spell of a communal mind. Although her "usual procedure was to keep away from gossip, from loose tongues," (Burns 107), she generally fails to do so. The social mind has an inflexible nature: "these people never backed off. That was their reputation, their hallmark, their stock-in-trade unstoppability" (Burns 240). The public opinion "invested in conjecture" (Burns 173) through its agents from different parts of the community.

The distinguishing characteristic of the narrator's memory in *Milkman* is its public aspect. Her mind includes the consciousness of a time moulded by the racial, religious, and "political problems" which she "did not like to get into" (Burns 26). After about two decades, she tries to show how being herself in such a time and place was impossible. Her narrative is the account of her toiling during hard times in which life and minds functioned based on "revenge and counter-revenge" (Burns 113).

The massive impact of rumours and gossip in the unnamed community in *Milkman* is a defining factor both in the narrator's memories and in her acts of remembering. For example, although she was a victim of the Milkman's assaults, she doubted her own certainty by asking herself whether there was really something between her and Milkman: "Certainly it felt to me that this milkman had done something, that he was about to do something, that strategically he was working up to some action. I think too — otherwise why all this gossip?" (Burns 64). The inflexible nature of the rumour and gossip-ridden society makes her disappointed. In other words, the social mind's ultimate truth is framed by rumour and gossip: "As for the rumour of me and the milkman, why should it be down to me to dispel it, to refute gossip by people who fostered gossip and clearly wouldn't welcome either, denial of their gossip?" (Burns 65) Although the narrator's reading-while-walking habit was considered by the social mind to be an uncommon and untraditional behaviour and by engaging in it she was "losing touch in a crucial sense with communal up-to-dateness" as it kept her away from the circulation of the social mind's rumours and gossip, it was her intentional action to take such a risk to keep herself away from the communal habit of rumours and gossip because in her community not knowing was safer than knowing. In her community, as she comments, "Knowledge didn't guarantee power, safety or relief and often for some it meant the opposite of power, safety and relief […] Purposely not wanting to know therefore, was exactly what my reading-while-walking was about. It was a vigilance not to be vigilant" (Burns 65).

The narrator's acts of remembering are all about a time when "social regularity" (Enright 60) was the basis of the social mind's judgements. She also tells us about a time when "it was best […] to keep the lowest of low profiles rather than admit your personal distinguishing habits" (Burns 60), and "the community […] had moved things on to the tune of the political problems" (Burns 61). Most of her acts of remembering are about the difficulty of surviving in a community where people rarely recognized her problems. For example, she did not know how to speak about her problems as nobody could understand her, including her maybe-boyfriend. Therefore, her storytelling includes reiterations "of [her] trying to explain [her problems] only to be misunderstood, or of trying to explain only not to be taken seriously" (Burns 64).

The overall plot turns around her inability to "speak of" the Milkman-caused "dilemma" she "found" herself in (Burns 64). In remembering her predicament, she comes to some conclusions: "It was that I didn't speak to anybody of anything — partly because I wasn't used to telling anybody anything, partly because I didn't know how to tell or what to tell, partly too, because still it was unclear there was anything of accuracy to tell. What had he done after all?" (Burns 64) The social mind in her community was incapable of understanding the nature of Milkman's harassment since it was a kind of psychological and non-physical torture: "Thing was, he hadn't physically touched me. Nor that last time had he even looked at me. So where was my premise for speaking out on how, uninvited, he was pushing in? But that was what it was like here. Everything had to be physical, had to be intellectually reasonable in order to be comprehensible" (Burns 64). Similarly, her third brother-in-law was mentally incapable of imagining and believing in any non-physical harassment: "brother-in-law would be incapable of believing that anything that wasn't physical between two people could, in fact, be going on" (Burns 64). Despite such a similarity, third brother-in-law was "diagnosed by the community" with a "mental aberration" as "he expected women to be doughty, inspirational, even mythical, supernatural figures" (Burns 12).

In her acts of remembering, the narrator presents a highly superstitious society wherein "keenness and initiative get stifled [...], turned to discouragement, twisted too, into darker channels" (Burns 147). It was widely divided between the modern generation's style of living and that of the older ones. The increasing division in the narrator's community is symbolically portrayed through her memory of the red-light street "where young couples went to live together who didn't want to get married or conventionally to settle down [...] unmarried couples lived there. It was even rumoured two men lived there, I mean together [...] There weren't any women living together, though one woman was famously said to live in number twenty-three with two men" (Burns 42). The closed minds in the narrator's community were not only against the people who lived in the red-light street, they were generally the enemy of the "shining people" in their environment (Burns 90). Remembering a film she watched when she was twelve years old, the narrator tries to show how being kind and goodhearted was impossible in her society where people:

> couldn't cope with being liked, couldn't cope with innocence, frankness, openness, with a defencelessness and an affection and purity so pure, so affectionate, that the dog and its qualities had to be done away with. Couldn't bear it. Had to kill it. [...] these people could not, not at the drop of a hat, be open to any bright shining button of a person stepping into their environment and shining upon them just like that. (Burns 89)

In her remembering, the narrator underscores the growing nature of her realization. In a deeper and broader sense, she comes to new realizations about her own role in becoming who she was both at the time of experiencing her memories and narrating them. Thus, she evaluates her identity and function in the time of experience from the perspective of the public mind in the contexts of her younger and older selves. Realization of the crossing or overlapping line between the two moulding factors of her identity is the main by-product of her narration. In other words, despite the sheer contrast between her own mind and the social minds, her narration reveals some similarities between the two as, from a detached perspective, she notices the shared point between her and the social mind's opposing perspectives. She surprisingly recognizes how sometimes the gossips about her turned out to be true.

The narrator in *Milkman* tries to justify her "closed-upness" by arguing that it was a ubiquitous behaviour since "everybody kept their private thoughts safe and sound in those recesses underneath" (Burns 91). Therefore, her closed-upness was a collective behaviour: "In those days then, impossible it was not to be closed-up because closed-upness was everywhere: closings in our community, closings in their community, the state here closed, the government 'over there' closed, the newspapers and radio and television closed because no information could be forthcoming that wouldn't be perceived by at least one party to be a distortion of the truth" (Burns 114). Besides constantly being threatened by the social mind's invisible judgements, the narrator was also physically threatened by "Being photographed" (Burns 66) on the streets, where "On each occasion when I did hear them, the camera would snap as I passed and so, yes, it seemed I'd fallen into some grid, maybe the central grid, as part of the disease, the rebel-infection" (Burns 66). Thus, the narrator shows how she devised some techniques which helped her survive in a gossip-ridden closed-up society. She tried to "keep safe" by hardly mentioning "anything to anybody" since, by intentionally being sucked in, she "wanted to stay as sane in [her] mind" as possible by buying and reading old books (Burns 44 and 115).

As a result of the social mind's demanding behaviour, she gradually undergoes a mental and emotional transformation. The integrity of her character disappears when she finds out that she failed to deceive the public mind by wearing protective masks: "my feelings stopped expressing. Then they stopped existing. And now this numbance from nowhere had come so far on in its development that along with others in the area finding me inaccessible, I, too, came to find me inaccessible. My inner world, it seemed, had gone away" (Burns 178).

The narrator's acts of remembering include her acknowledgements. For example, by saying "[It] took me a while to realise I too, was on that list," she remembers how she finally recognized the way the social mind "branded" her a "psychological misfit" or one of the "beyond-the-pale[s]" (Burns 60). When she finds out that she failed to deceive the social mind, she blames herself for her role in her own destruction: "Too late I realised that all the time I'd been an active player, a contributing element, a major componential in the downfall of myself" (Burns 178). She also becomes disappointed to see that her attempts to "confound" gossips were useless and ineffective since the people in her community "didn't care for confoundment and complained that my demeanour was improper, that it was resistant to ordinary treatment, that it was against the common weal, that I was almost-inordinately blank, almost-lifeless, almost-sterile, almost-counter-intuitive which was not and couldn't ever be, they said, normal for a person on this earth ceaselessly to be" (Burns 179). As the narrator finds out towards the end of her storytelling, her silence regarding "sexual pursuit and sexual stalking" (Burns 183) not only did not protect her, but also made her more susceptible to sexual harassment and violence. As a result of her silence about her problems, her mother and sister, whose perspective represented that of the social minds, put more pressure on her by censuring her about her relationship with the Milkman. Her taciturn nature also heightens the "tension" between herself and her boyfriend. Instead of directly talking about the threat to herself and to her maybe-boyfriend on the part of the Milkman, she indirectly tries to protect him against the Milkman's possible threats. In this way, she lives inside a possible world built by her own mentality which is consolidated in her character by the constantly renewing train of rumours and gossips.

Therefore, in her acts of remembering, the narrator comes to the conclusion that she is also partly to blame for her painful experience as her strict self-reservedness and "lack of certainty" (Burns 181) contributed to the communal misunderstanding of her. She simply did not know the codes of her society: "I didn't know how to approach these guys [the paramilitaries]" (Burns 182). Besides the role of her community in her situation, her antisocial mode of life also enhanced her sense of sociocultural detachment. As a result of the primary impact of her situation on her perspective towards her community, she did intentionally "withhold" herself from the other people, and this enhanced the "communal drain" upon her "by the community" (Burns 181). Thus, in her account, she regrets that her intentional choice of isolation:

> Had I really been as stubborn and transverse and as ten-minute area as all of the reprehenders of me had said I had? Looking back, and excluding my friendship with my one remaining trusted-fewest person from schooldays, I think too, that yes, I had. My distrust had been phenomenal to the point where I could not see that probably there had existed individuals who could have helped, who might have supported and comforted me. (Burns 181)

She overcomes her sense of "fear" and feels brave after Milkman's death. Having been emboldened by his death as it was thought that her "protection was now dead" (Burns 306), when Somebody McSomebody threatens her to death by putting his gun to her head in the toilets of a drinking club, as she remembers, she "snapped the gun off him" and by doing so she "offered a different perspective, a freeing-up of the fear option" (Burns 309). As an effect of "freeing-up of the fear," she picks up her usual walking and running although she knew that she should not do reading-while-walking as it was an unconventional (Burns 312). On the narrator's journey towards peace and tranquillity, however, there were enormous obstacles which were fuelled by the spread of rumours and gossips. Similarly, they intended to (re)define the narrator's identity.

The most effective agent of the rumours and gossips in her own family was her first brother-in-law. The narrator remembers him as "a piece of dirt" whose "predatory nature pushed [her] into frozenness every time" (Burns 2). Eight years before being exposed to the Milkman's harassment, the narrator had been an object of her first brother-in-law's teasing and "lewd remarks" (Burns 2). The narrator's acts of remembering of her experience with her brother-in-law in the past are traumatic and embarrassing: "In his compulsions he made things up about other people's sexlives. About my sexlife. When I was younger, when I was twelve [...he] felt entitled to make his remarks and I did not speak because I did not know how to respond to this person" (Burns 1-2). Despite the fact that "twenty-three years' difference" (Burns 2) between the narrator and Milkman was exactly the same as it had been between her and her first brother-in-law in the past, he started and spread rumours about her relationship with Milkman by highlighting the big age difference.

Milkman's massive contribution to the plot structure in Burns's narrative is obvious from its name. *Milkman* is primarily about Milkman. In the same way, the narrator's acts of remembering are firstly about Milkman: "I was being talked about because there was a rumour started by them, or more likely by first brother-in-law, that I had been having an affair with this milkman and that I was eighteen and he was forty-one" (Burns 1). He is everywhere in her different embedded narratives. The unnamed narrator's "confusion," "shock" (Burns 10), and intense suffering inflicted on her by the mysterious man's presence constitute the foundation of her acts of remembering.

Acting as the symbol of the narrator's community, the "omniscient," and "sinister" Milkman (Burns 106) is presented as an emblem of evil. The narrator describes him as a "notorious man" (Burns 299), as a "solemn, austere" (Burns 144) person "Much older" but "more assured" than herself (Burns 135), and as a person who had "infiltrated [her] psyche" (Burns 166). His violence against her is a tacit kind since "There was no overt sense [...] that he could be transgressing" (Burns 136). However, the narrator's overall storytelling activity is about his steady "encroachments" upon her (Burns 170). He appears in the narrator's acts of remembering in the figure of a big brother, silently "pursuing and importuning" her (Burns 54), following her everywhere, knowing everything about her, and even reading her mind. She uses her reading-while-walking habit and walking with her third brother-in-law as a "deterrent" (Burns 58) to keep "milkman away" although she becomes disappointed as he "switch[es] tactics" (Burns 78).

Milkman is presented as a ubiquitous threat in the storyworld. The way he "startled" the narrator by offering a lift to her while she "was walking along reading *Ivanhoe*" (Burns 3) also startles the reader. Although she politely rejected his offer and "had not been having an affair with the milkman [...] and had been frightened and confused by his pursuing" (Burns 1), the rumours and gossips about them immediately spread: "Seemed my lover was a milkman, they said—though also they said he was a motor mechanic. He was in his early forties, they said—though also round about his twenties. He was married, they said—also not married. Definitely he was 'connected'—though 'unconnected' at the same time. An intelligence officer" (Burns 48). Accordingly, the rapid spread of gossip about the narrator's alleged inappropriate relationship with Milkman redefines her relationship with people from the inside and outside of her family.

Her mental "preoccupation with the milkman" (Burns 14) brings about a physically and mentally self-confined life for her in such a way that it does not leave any place for her life as an adolescent. For example, she cannot focus on her maybe-boyfriend: "I myself was keeping a look-out for the disturbance even though I did not want that person in my head. I wanted maybe boyfriend in my head, for there he'd been, all cosy, until uneasiness about the milkman had pushed him out of it" (Burns 15-16). In other words, the unexpected appearance of Milkman fundamentally changes the outward and inward orders in her life.

Milkman's mostly nonverbal harassment continues although in their meetings he "asked nothing" of her nor "physically touch[ed]" her (Burns 6). These events trigger the ever-spreading rumours and gossips about the nature of a relationship between an older man a younger girl: "The scandal of this milkman affair had mushroomed to the point where it was now rabid and raging and fast becoming a best-seller and because of it, because of all those compounding violations, I was finding myself more and more circumscribed into an incoherent, debilitated place" (Burns 170).

In remembering her Milkman-related memories, the narrator criticises her passive reaction against his bold pushing: "Why could I just not stop this running and tell this man to leave me alone?

Apart from 'where did he come from?' I didn't have those other thoughts until later, and I don't mean an hour later. I mean twenty years later" (Burns 6). She immediately tries to justify her reaction through admitting to her own deficiencies and ignorance when she was eighteen: "At eighteen I had no proper understanding of the ways that constituted encroachment. I had a feeling for them, an intuition, a sense of repugnance for some situations and some people, but I did not know intuition and repugnance counted, did not know I had a right not to like, not to have to put up with, anybody and everybody coming near" (Burns 6). The narrator, however, takes away responsibility for her closed behaviour and its consequences for herself by highlighting the male and female territory in her community: "I could not be fitter than this man, could not be more knowledgeable about my own regime than this man, because the conditioning of males and females here would never have allowed that. This was the 'I'm male and you're female' territory" (Burns 7-8).

In the absence of meaningful verbal communication between the two, she contends that mindreading acted as a main medium of interaction between them. By having the first-person narrative advantage, the narrator in her acts of remembering shows how she tried to understand his thoughts and motives through mindreading: "I knew he knew that finally I'd grasped what it was he was saying to me" (Burns 116). Or, in a similar other situation, she says, "impossible it was not to grasp what he was dropping big hints about. I did grasp. I drew the allusion, made the underpinnings" (Burns 168). Likewise, as she admits, her mindreading was her only device to use against Milkman's efforts to find out her "intentions" through "mind-reading" (Burns 135). When he sees her after she comes out of French night class and wrongly asks, "'At your Greek and Roman Class, were you?'" (Burns 103), the narrator uses his wrong question as a clue to the Milkman's knowledge as well as to his intentions about her:

> That meant the milkman got it wrong and I didn't correct him for getting it wrong because it gave me hope that in the middle of his knowing everything he didn't know everything. [...] This struck me as eerie, indicative too, of a thorough research carried out by a man who gleaned, docketed and filed

> each and every bit of information, even if on this occasion he mistook the outcome in the end. (Burns 103)

Her experiences in the second meeting with the Milkman embolden the narrator. Through following the clues in his words on their third visit, she tries to understand his knowledge and thoughts about herself. It is painful to her to know that Milkman "knew" (Burns 105) a lot of things about her maybe-boyfriend: "He knew maybe-boyfriend's house, his district, also his name, who his mates were, where he worked, even that he used to work in that car factory that had to close that time with the entire workforce made redundant. He knew too, that I slept with maybe-boyfriend" (Burns 105). Based on her initial mindreading and as it "appeared [to her] to be underlined by [...] milkman in the subsoil of [their] conversation," she concludes that "maybe-boyfriend was to be killed under the catch-all of the political problems even if, in reality, the milkman was going to kill him out of disguised sexual jealousy over me. Such appeared to be underlined by this milkman in the subsoil of our conversation" (Burns 115). Being gripped by the thought that Milkman would hurt maybe-boyfriend, her anxiety and restlessness increase in a way that she thinks Milkman is following them everywhere:

> "while downtown at the bars and clubs with maybe-boyfriend, I'd find myself glancing around, anxious that the milkman might be in here with us. I thought he might be watching us, spying on us, perhaps taking secret pictures of us, and especially I'd be worried" (Burns 168).

Milkman pushes her into an abstract state of in-betweenness in a way that she submitted herself to his orders readily: "defeated, I'd surrender and step voluntarily as his woman into his vehicles, I wasn't sure anymore what was plausible, what was exaggeration, what might be reality or delusion or paranoia. Wouldn't have occurred to me either, that cultivating helplessness and a growing mental dispossession might all be part of this man's world of stimulation too" (Burns 169). Having discovered the romantic bond between maybe-boyfriend and the chef, when she comes out their house, Milkman gives her a ride. She remembers her ultimate submission to the Milkman's desires: "there was no choice. It was that there was no more alternative. Ill-equipped I'd been to take in what everybody else from the outset easily had taken in: I was Milkman's fait accompli all along" (Burns 299).

The narrator's memory of the moment her elder sister gave her the news of Milkman's death (Chapter Seven) is an illustrative example of the role of her mental ability in reading other people's thoughts, intentions, and goals. She vividly remembers how her sister "scanned [her] face to see how [she] would take it [the Milkman's death]" (Burns 301). Based on the facial expression of her sister, she does her mindreading: "She thinks this [the Milkman's death] will teach me a lesson, I thought." Thus, she reads her intentions based on her evaluation: "This was everything to do with her not wanting me to have what long ago she had stopped allowing herself [...] She continued to look transported, far from that state of grief she'd been walking about in for ages" (Burns 301).

Milkman's death brought about some realizations in the narrator as well as in the public mind. After his death, suddenly the "consensus" in the public was that his name was "'An unusual name'" as it "broke bounds of credibility." Thus, the news of his death "unsettled people; it cheated them, frightened them and there seemed no way round a feeling of embarrassment either" (Burns 305). Milkman's greatness disappears in the public eye in a short time:

> When considered a pseudonym, some codename, 'the milkman' had possessed mystique, intrigue, theatrical possibility. Once out of symbolism, however, once into the everyday, the banal [...] any respect it had garnered as the cognomen of a high-cadre paramilitary activist was undercut immediately and, just as immediately, fell away. (Burns 305)

When her elder sister happily gave her the news of Milkman's death, although not expressed in words, her whole body proclaimed a sense of happiness as "relief was coursing through" her (Burns 302) because of his death. However, because of the social mind, she hides her true feelings carefully: "On hearing the news, and even in the privacy of the subtext of my own mind where nobody but me could witness me being me, also out of fear of being judged in the area some traitorous, cold-hearted bad person, I myself was trying not to be happy" (Burns 304). In reviewing the impact of Milkman's life and death on her own life, she comes to some realisations: "I came to understand how much I'd been closed down, how much I'd been thwarted into a carefully constructed nothingness by that man. Also by the community, by the very mental atmosphere, that minutiae of invasion" (Burns 303).

The unnameable narrator's storytelling in *Milkman* is, thus, both a historical and a biographical account. Through her reliable manner of acts of remembering and recollections, on the one hand she celebrates the ending of a dark era in her community. On the other hand, by reviewing her biography, she shares with us of the way she could survive in a troubled community which was against women, change, and freedom of action, expression, and thought.

# FIVE
# CONCLUSION

The narrators' identification with memory is a salient shared thematic focus in *The Sea*, *The Gathering*, and *Milkman*. They are retrospective narratives of perception, confession, and experiential memory. The narrators in these narratives are consciously recollecting or recalling some events they experienced at particular times in the past. Narration of memory in these narratives is used as an effective device in the narrators' battle against their mental breakdowns and depressions. Their conscious process of recollection provides them with the opportunity to overcome the negative impact of some traumatic episodes from their past lives.

As we have seen in the foregoing chapters, storytelling activity in the narratives examined in this book is based on episodic memory which, in Mark A. Wheeler's words, "is defined by the nature of conscious awareness that accompanies retrieval, a type of awareness now called autonoetic (self-knowing) awareness" (597). In a self-reflective manner, the narrators in *The Sea*, *The Gathering*, and *Milkman* mentally travel through time, and relentlessly concentrate on detailed description of episodes from their past. Hence, they are memory-oriented narratives. The heavy burden of remembering is highlighted in these narratives. The narrators of these narratives are caught up with some of their experiences as they are unable to forget some of the events they experienced in the past. Therefore, their recollective experiences are recounted in order to help them come to terms with what they cannot forget. Their acts of remembering also inform their identities and their connection with other characters.

Storying the past is the shared narrative concern in *The Sea*, *The Gathering*, and *Milkman*. The present in these narratives is intertwined with the past which is the controller of the character-narrator's consciousness. The examination of the past brings about their understanding of why and how what happened in the past, happened. As a result of their (mis)acts of remembering, memory formations, (un)real memories, and recollections/retellings/ (re)constrictions, they come to some realizations about their own particular identities and those of others.

The narrator's storytelling activities include both factual and fictional memories. They recount what they remember and what they seem to remember. In other words, besides recounting their recollected memories, the narrators also share their discourse of metamemory, or their judgements about memory as a mental system. The memory presented in their narratives lacks authenticity and reliability. Rather, it is elusive, fragmented, unreliable, deceiving, fraudulent, subject to time, or prone to change and reformation. Retold acts of memories, therefore, are mostly (re)constructed acts. The rememberers in their autobiographical narratives in *The Sea*, *The Gathering*, and *Milkman* combine what they remember from the past events with what they add to the missing parts. Their memories are, therefore, a constructed memory—as much real as unreal or fake.

Memory is also represented as the most defining element of identity in *The Sea*, *The Gathering*, and *Milkman*. In other words, memory in these narratives is represented as an identity-defining quality, or identity is a narrative-dependent denominator. Memory is central to the tensions about which the narrators tell their stories. Remembering is used as a metaphor for both traumatic experience and as a process for creating a sense of identity. To be supportive of the narrators in these narratives is equally being supportive of memory. Memory is closely annexed to their sense of personal and cultural identity. Memory is, however, an incomplete phenomenon which is constantly under (re)construction and cultivation. It is mostly an evasive and prone-to-disappearing factor of identity. By the end of their storytelling, the narrators present more positive and coherent selves.

The main goal of the narrators' acts of remembering is their own mental and psychological need and treatment. At the early stage of their storytelling, they all have unquiet minds. They remember, recount, and/or imagine some eventful episodes in their past lives in order to remind themselves of what they once lived, and to come to terms with the long-term impact of the related events on their minds. Thus, their autobiographical narration is designed to help them go beyond the painful events, and, if possible, even forget them. The narrators, thus, are oscillating between remembering and forgetting. However, they are conscious of their unavoidable need to construct memory wherever it fails to provide them with a persuasive picture of the past.

The death of a close person brings about spontaneous outpourings of the narrators' memories in *The Sea*, *The Gathering*, and *Milkman*. Their storytelling activities, therefore, act as a reaction to a quite terrible situation. Their stories move between past and present times. Memory in these narratives is presented as experience. They represent the way the narrators hold on to their memories to re-experience and imagine what happened in the past. The narrators relate some significant events they personally experienced at particular times in particular places in their past. Through combining recollection with imagination, the narrators present an emancipating version of the past in their narratives. Therefore, their storyworld is a universe of relativities.

The narrator's autobiographical narration in John Banville's *The Sea* is a self-examination through which he tries to make his life worth living. Max Morden's act of storytelling has generally two goals. First, *Nosce te ipsum* (know thyself) lies at the centre of his acts of remembering. He tells his life story in order to know himself by reviewing the construction process of his own sense of identity. In addition, his remembering is the pillar of his sense of identity and being. He tries to maintain the dead people's images in his mind as much as possible because losing a person's memory for him equals that person's real death, disappearance, or annihilation. Therefore, he tries to remember, and wherever needed to pretend to remember, the defining episodes of past life as he does not want his mind to fade into oblivion.

Similarly, the dichotomy of constructed or fabricated memory and the historical version of it makes up the narrative fiction in Anne Enright's *The Gathering*, where the border between reality and fiction is blurred. In her use of storytelling as a medium of constructing the past, Enright's narrator crosses the line between memory and imagination. Her primary goal of narration is to find out the truth about herself and the other characters. Since her acts of remembering fail to retrieve the realties about the events and people in the past, Veronica uses her own imaginings to make up for the shortcomings of her memory. Thus, her storytelling includes both acts of narration and disnarration of memories, or recounting events that happened and/or did not happen in the past. In this way, she discovers the truth through her distant and vague memories by relying on the possibilities. Her storytelling, therefore, brings about a resolution to a past event, on the one hand, and, on the other hand, it clears up her confusion to some extent in such a way that, on the horizon, she feels a new soul is appearing in her body. Thus, thanks to her skill in storytelling, she experiences a development in her sense of identity as she is motivated to resume the normal order of her life at the end of her narrative.

The plot in Anna Burns's *Milkman* also depends on memory and acts of remembering. In her autobiography, the unnamed narrator highlights her identity problem. The established order of the patriarchal society and the invisible threats imposed on the narrator-character as an unusually interesting woman in the horrific time of national unrest are presented in *Milkman* as the two main causes of her conflicts. She remembers how as a female citizen her identity was under erasure in the time of terror. Her memories are full with a sense of fear, insecurity, psychological pressure, conflicts as much as with realizations, learnings and changes. Through her different embedded narratives, the narrator shows how the few recounted months acted in her life as a school where she learned about the socio-cultural realities of her community before managing to resume her normal life at the end. Thus, although she had some traumatic and painful experiences, they all led to a happy state—Milkman was shot, she reconciled with her mother, she discovered the truth about her maybe-boyfriend and the chef, and she resumed her running habit via her third brother-in-law. Storytelling in *Milkman*, therefore, acts as a celebration for the narrator. After about two decades and through remembering some constructive episodes from her past life, she feels happy to be living in a different communal context. She feels emancipated in postmillennial Irish society which has overcome some difficult cultural and political obstacles in its near past.

*The Sea*, *The Gathering*, and *Milkman* show the significance of memory, remembering, and identity. Likewise, the narratives highlight the centrality of storytelling acts and their balancing function in individuals' lives. The narrators in these narratives do not try to numb, avoid, or deny what they experienced; instead, they endeavour to better understand and work through their unsettling episodic memories by recollecting, remembering, and/or storying them. As it turns out towards the end of their acts of remembering, the narrators' storytelling activities help them come to terms with their sense of grief for their losses in the past as well as enrich their self-awareness and realisation in a similar way to what Fireman et al. highlight: "The stories we tell to ourselves and others, for ourselves and others, are a central means by which we come to know ourselves and others, thereby enriching our conscious awareness" (3). Likewise, the most important return in these narratives is enrichment of the narrators', as well as our, consciousnesses.

# WORKS CITED

Albright, Daniel. "Literary and Psychological Models of the Self." *The Remembering Self: Construction and Accuracy in the Self Narrative*, edited by Ulric Neisser and Robyn Fivush. Cambridge University Press, 1994, pp. 19-40.

Baddeley, Alan. "What is Autobiographical Memory." *Theoretical Perspectives on Autobiographical Memory*, edited by Martin A. Conway et al. Springer-Netherlands, 1992, pp. 13-30.

Banville, John. *The Sea*. Picador, 2005.

Barnes, Julian. *Elizabeth Finch*. Alfred A. Knof, 2022.

Benjamin, Walter. *The Storyteller Essays*. Translated from the German by Tess Lewis, edited and with an introduction by Samuel Titan, New York Review of Books, 2019.

Berntsen, Dorthe and David C. Rubin. "Introduction." *Understanding Autobiographical Memory: Theories and Approaches*, edited by Dorthe Berntsen and David C. Rubin. Cambridge University Press, 2012, pp. 1-8.

— "Understanding Autobiographical Memory: An Ecological Theory." *Understanding Autobiographical Memory: Theories and Approaches*, edited by Dorthe Berntsen and David C. Rubin. Cambridge University Press, 2012, pp. 333-355.

Bledsoe, Eric Matthew. "'Make It New'." *The Routledge Encyclopaedia of Modernism*. Taylor and Francis, 2016, doi: 10.4324/9781135000356-REM1131-1. Date Accessed 16 Feb. 2022.

Bergson, Henri. *Creative Mind*: *An Introduction to Metaphysics*. Translated by Mabelle L. Andison. New York: Dover Publications Inc, 2007.

Brockmeier, Jens. "Remembering and Forgetting: Narrative as Cultural Memory." *Culture & Psychology*, Vol. 8(1): 15—43, 2002.

Cahill, Susan. "Post-Millennial Irish Fiction." *The Oxford Handbook of Modern Irish Fiction*, edited by Liam Harte, Oxford University Press, 2020, pp. 603-619.

Costello-Sullivan, Kathleen. "Trauma and Recovery in the post-Celtic Tiger Period: Recuperating the Parent-Child Bond in Contemporary Irish Fiction." *Routledge International Handbook of Irish Studies*, edited by Renée Fox, Mike Cronin, and Brian Ó Conchubhair. New York: Routledge, 2021, pp. 407-419.

— *Trauma and Recovery in the Twenty-First-Century Irish Novel.* Syracuse: Syracuse University Press, 2018.

Deina, Maria-Adriana. "Feel the Trouble(s) Around You: Sensing the Everyday Politics of Conflict through Anna Burns' *Milkman.*" *Political Anthropological Research on International Social Sciences*, vol. 3, no. 1, 2022, pp. 29—39, doi: 10.1163/25903276-bja10034. Date Accessed 14 Dec. 2022.

Dell'Amico, Carol. "Anne Enright's "The Gathering": Trauma, Testimony, Memory." *New Hibernia Review / Iris Éireannach Nua*, vol. 14, no. 3, 2010, pp. 59-74, https://www.jstor.org/stable/20779266. Accessed 8 February 2022.

Derek, Hand. "John Banville and the Idea of the Precursor: Some Meditations." *John Banville and His Precursors*, edited by Pietra Palazzolo, Michael Springer and Stephen Butler. London: Bloomsbury Academic, 2019, pp. 17-33.

Drong, Leszek. "Remembering a Transcultural Past: Recent Post-Tribal Fictions of Seventies Ardoyne." *Critique: Studies in Contemporary Fiction*, vol. 61, no. 2, 2020, pp. 171-180, https://doi.org/10.1080/00111619.2019.1687416. Accessed 19 April 2022.

Eliot, T. S. "Hamlet." *Selected Essays*, London: Faber and Faber, 1932.

Ender, Evelyne. *Architexts of Memory: Literature, Science, and Autobiography*. The University of Michigan Press, 2005.

English, Bridget. *Laying Out the Bones: Death and Dying in the Modern Irish Novel*. Syracuse: Syracuse University Press, 2017.

Enright, Anne. *The Gathering*. London: Vintage, 2008.

Erll, Astrid. "Narratology and Cultural Memory Studies." *Narratology in the Age of Cross-Disciplinary Narrative Research*, edited by Sandra Heinen and Roy Sommer. Walter de Gruyter, 2009, pp. 212-227.

Erll, Astrid and Ansgar Nünning. "Where Literature and Memory Meet: Towards a Systematic Approach to the Concept of Memory Used in Literary Studies." *Real 21: Literature, Literary History, and Cultural Memory*, edited by Herbert Grabes. Gunter Narr Verlag Tübingen, 2005, pp. 261-294.

Estévez-Saá, Margarita. "Recent Contributions to the Irish Novel by Sara Baume, Anna Burns and Eleanor O'Reilly: On Language, Words and Wordlessness." *Oceánide*, vol. 13, 2022, pp. 85-94, https://doi.org/10.37668/oceanide.v13i.44. Accessed 8 January 2023.

Fiorato, Sidia. *The Relationship between Literature and Science in John Banville's Scientific Tetralogy*. Peter Lang, 2007.

Fireman, Gary D., Ted E. McVay Jr. and Owen Flanagan. "Introduction." *Narrative and*

*Consciousness: Literature, Psychology, and the Brain*, edited by Gary D. Fireman Ted E. McVay, Jr. and Owen J. Flanagan. Oxford University Press, 2003, pp. 3-16

Ganteau, Jean Michel. "Remembrance Between Act and Event: Anne Enright's *The Gathering*." *Traumatic Memory and the Ethical, Political and Transhistorical Functions of Literature*, edited by Susana Onega, Constanza del Río and Maite Escudero-Alías. Palgrave Macmillan, 2017, pp. 181.200.

Grmusa, Lovorka Gruic and Biljana Oklopcic. *Memory and Identity in Modern and Postmodern American Literature*. Gateway East (Singapore): Springer Nature Singapore Pte Ltd, 2022.

Guidarini, Lisa. "An interview with Colm Tóibín." *Bluestalking*, https://bluestalkingjournal.com/2014/04/10/an-interview-with-colm-toibin/. Accessed 14 October 2022.

Hansson, Heidi. "Anne Enright and Postnationalism in the Contemporary Irish Novel." *Irish literature since 1990: diverse voices*, edited by Scott Brewster and Michael Parker. Manchester: Manchester University Press, 2009, pp. 216-231.

Harte, Liam. "Modern Irish Fiction: Renewing the Art of the New." *The Oxford Handbook of Modern Irish Fiction*, edited by Liam Harte, Oxford University Press, 2020, pp. 3-46.

— *Reading the Contemporary Irish Novel: 1987–2007*. Chichester: Wiley Blackwell, 2014.

Hutton, Clare. "The Moment and Technique of Milkman." *Essays in Criticism*, vol. 69, no. 3, 2021, pp. 349-371, https://doi.org/10.1215/00166928-8911537. Accessed 24 May 2022.

Jordan, Justine. "A new Irish literary boom: the post-crash stars of fiction." *The Guardian*, 17 Oct. 2015, https://www.theguardian.com/books/2015/oct/17/new-irish-literary-boom-post-crash-stars-fiction. Accessed 16 Feb. 2022. Accessed 26 October 2022.

King, Nicola. *Memory, Narrative, Identity: Remembering the Self*. Edinburgh University Press, 2000.

Lachmann, Renate. "Mnemonic and Intertextual Aspects of Literature." *Cultural Memory Studies: An International and Interdisciplinary Handbook*, edited by Astrid Erll and Ansgar Nünning. Walter de Gruyter, 2008, pp. 301-310.

Linde, Charlotte. "Memory in Narrative." *The International Encyclopaedia of Language and Social Interaction*, First Edition, edited by Karen Tracy (General Editor), Cornelia Ilie and Todd Sandel (Associate Editors). John Wiley & Sons, 2015, pp. 1-9.

Locke, John. *An Essay Concerning Human Understanding*. Edited by Peter H. Midditch, Oxford: Clarendon Press, 1975.

Martínez-Alfaro, María Jesús and Silvia Pellicer-Ortín. "Introduction: Memory Frictions—Conflict—Negotiation—Politics in Contemporary Literature in English." *Memory Frictions in Contemporary Literature*, edited by María Jesús Martínez-Alfaro and Silvia Pellicer-Ortín. Palgrave McMillan, 2017, pp.1-17.

McCarthy, Karen. "A Fool's Errand: Blanchot, Mourning and *The Sea*." *John Banville and His Precursors*, edited by Pietra Palazzolo, Michael Springer and Stephen Butler. London: Bloomsbury Academic, 2019, pp. 165-176.

McSweeney, Kerry. ""David Copperfield" and the Music of Memory." *Dickens Studies Annual*, vol. 23, 1994, pp. 93-119, https://www.jstor.org/stable/44371860. Accessed 12 March 2022.

McWilliams, Ellen. *Women and Exile in Contemporary Irish Fiction*. Hampshire: Palgrave Macmillan, 2013.

Murphy, Neil. "John Banville's Fictions of Art." *The Oxford Handbook of Modern Irish Fiction,* edited by Liam Harte. Oxford: Oxford University Press, 2020, pp. 320-334.

Neumann, Bright. "The Literary Representation of Memory." *Cultural Memory Studies: An International and Interdisciplinary Handbook*, edited by Astrid Erll and Ansgar Nünning. Walter de Gruyter, 2008, pp. 333-343.

O'Connell, Mark. *John Banville's Narcissistic Fictions*. New York: Palgrave Macmillan, 2013.

O'Toole, Fintan. "Irish Society and Culture in the Twenty-First Century." *ABEI Journal: The Brazilian Journal of Irish Studies*, no. 11, 2009, pp. 99-109.

Palmer, Alan. *Social Minds in the Novel*. Columbus: the Ohio State University Press, 2010.

Patten, Eva. "Contemporary Irish Fiction." *The Cambridge Companion to the Irish Novel*, edited by John Wilson Foster. Cambridge: Cambridge University Press, 2006, pp. 259-275.

Piątek, Beata. "The "Unspeakableness" of Life in Northern Ireland: Anna Burns's Milkman." *Litteraria Copernicana*, vol. 3, no. 35, 2020, pp. 105-114, http://dx.doi.org/10.12775/LC.2020.039. Accessed 28 February 2021.

Rubin, David C. "Introduction." *Remembering Our Past: Studies in Autobiographical Memory*, edited by Rubin David C. Cambridge, Cambridge University Press, 1995, pp. 1-18.

Schmid, Wolf. *Mental Events: Changes of Mind in European Narratives from the Middle Ages to Postrealism*. Hamburg: Hamburg University Press, 2021.

Smorti, Andrea. *Telling to Understand: The Impact of Narrative on Autobiographical Memory*. Springer, 2018.

"Stavans, Ilan. "Memory and Literature." Translated from the Spanish by Brian G. Sheehy. *Agni*, no. 48, 1998, pp. 79-90. *JSTOR*, https://www.jstor.org/stable/23007941. Accessed 07 January 2021.

Trevor, William. *The Story of Lucy Gault*. London: Penguin Books, 2003.

Tulving, Endel. *Elements of Episodic Memory*. Oxford: Oxford University Press, 1983.

— "Episodic Memory: From Mind to Brain." *Annual Review of Psychology*, 2002, 53, 1-25.

Tulving, Endel and Fergus Craik. "Preface." *The Oxford Handbook of Memory*, edited by Endel Tulving and Fergus Craik, Oxford University Press, 2000, pp. v-ix.

Wagoner, Brady. "Introduction: Remembering as a Psychological and Social—Cultural Process." *Handbook of Culture and Memory*, edited by Brady Wagoner. Oxford: Oxford University Press, 2018, pp. 1-16.

Wheeler, Mark A. "Episodic Memory and Autonoetic Awareness." *The Oxford Handbook of Memory*, edited by Endel Tulving and Fergus Craik, Oxford University Press, 2000, pp. 597-608.

# About the Authors

**Naghmeh Varghaiyan** is a faculty member at the Department of English Language and Literature in Agri Ibrahim Cecen University, Türkiye. Her main research and teaching interests are in twentieth and twenty-first-century English Literature. Her work has appeared in various peer reviewed journals and edited collections. Her first book, *The Rhetoric of Women's Humour in Barbara Pym's Fiction*, was published in 2020.

**Karam Nayebpour** is a faculty member and the Head of English Language and Literature Department at Agri Ibrahim Cecen University, Türkiye. His research interests are Narratology and English Literature. Nayebpour is a member of European Narratology Network (ENN). He has published two books—*Interpersonal Relationships in George Eliot's The Mill on The Floss* (2017) and *Mind Presentation in Ian McEwan's Fiction and Fictional Minds* (2019). His work has also appeared in a number of journals and edited collections.

*ibidem*.eu